OTHER BOOKS BY JAY R. LEACH

How Should We Then Live
Behold the Man
The Blood Runs Through It
Drawn Away
Give Me Jesus
A Lamp unto My Feet
Grace that Saves
The Narrow Way
Radical Restoration in the Church
Manifestation of the true Children of God

MANIFESTATION OF THE TRUE CHILDREN OF GOD

EMBRACING THE RIGHTEOUSNESS OF GOD

JAY LEACH

Trafford rev. 05/21/2015

 www.trafford.com
North America & international
toll-free: 1 888 232 4444 (USA & Canada)
fax: 812 355 4082

CONTENTS

PART II
"WHAT WE DO"

THIS BOOK IS DEDICATED TO OUR LORD
AND
SAVIOR, JESUS CHRIST

INTRODUCTION

There was a time when truth mattered above all else. However, in these days of moral relativism and the new tolerance much of the true truth is being misinterpreted including the truth of God's Word. For example, love has replaced truth. Unity is more important than any doctrinal truth including the gospel of Jesus Christ and the Holy Spirit and His ministry. The heresy being, "it's better to tolerate than risk looking unloving to the world." God forbid!

Unfortunately, those of this persuasion chime, "to keep peace and harmony, doctrinal detours are permissible; and breaches of immorality are to be quickly forgiven. A mockery of God's moral law in the courts is accepted as progress. In spite of the sludge don't be dismayed by appearances, there are authentic communities of faith that are reaching increasing numbers of lost people and helping them grow into full and faithful children of God.

Yet, in spite of this present truth, some local churches and even some denominations chose to reject the redemptive work of Christ and the Great Commissions in God's redemptive plan. They just purr along year after year with well entrenched traditions, programs, flow-charts, and packaged presentations that have no place for the Holy Spirit's presence or guidance. These churches long ago gave up their main biblical purpose and calling [souls for Christ]!

My aim is to get rid of the shallowness in my life activities and get the transforming true truth of saving grace to everyone I can. Many children of God in their eighties claim they are just beginning to grasp the gospel. Being five years south of eighty years old myself, I believe that through Jesus Christ, the church remains the hope of the world; and the children of God need not make any apologies for striving to get better at what we "all" were called to do!

Not only must we be serious about helping people come to know Jesus Christ in a redemptive relational way, but we must also equip them to grow into mature Spirit-led children of God, shining representatives and truth bearers for Christ.

Too often we try to be expert witnesses for Christ in theory only, instead of being witnesses in our own right to what we have seen and experienced in our own lives through Him! Jesus promised,

> *"You shall receive power after the Holy Spirit has come upon you and you shall be My witnesses in Jerusalem, Judea and to the uttermost part of the earth"*
> *(Acts 1:8).*

Jesus passed that promise [of power to *witness*] on to the early church and the church today. Satan has tried to destroy the church of Jesus Christ before it could destroy him. His plan failed him miserably – for God had another plan! Rather than being destroyed, the early church arose in the *power of the Holy Spirit* and met the challenge with the *power of the gospel*, just as we will arise in our own day to meet any challenges the enemy will attempt to put on us. Equipped with "the whole armor of God" (see Ephesians 6:10-18), these early children of God lived victoriously for the Lord during the worst persecutions. Through Christ we can also rise up victoriously in our own day to meet any challenges Satan attempts to put before us! Remember, we carry the fight from victory – not to victory! Christ said from the Cross, "It is finished!" His death and resurrection defeated all foes; and gave us resurrection power to aid Him in the mock-up. The war is over! Salvation is available to the whole world (see John 3:16).

Church history has reported repeatedly how rapid and intense hatred for Christians grew for the early church; and now worldwide in this present age. It is inevitable that some of the extremes suffered by them will reach our shores unless God intervenes. America seems to not be very interested in God's provision, a promise that could prevent this coming flood (once again, carefully study 2 Chronicles 7:14). God has offered the cure for America through His people! He began the passage, *"If My people ...."* We should trust and obey Him! Chose to fervently pray like your life depended on it! The Scriptural "power of two or three" of His righteous children coming together in Christ's name still avails much. My intent in writing this book is to pass on proven principles that when applied will manifest the children of God who shine like His Son!

– Jay R. Leach
Bread of Life Ministries, Int'l
Whiteville, North Carolina

PART I

WHAT WE ARE

PART 1

WHAT WE ARE

SECTION ONE

THE KINGDOM AGENDA

CHAPTER 1

THE CHILDREN OF GOD

"...... in this are the children of God manifest ......"
(1 John 3:7-12).

Identity crises happen to people at various stages of their lives. Young people, especially those ages 11-34 [called millennials] agonize over a sense of purpose and direction for their lives. Mid-life is often a time of changing the directions previously set. Retirement forces the senior adult to find identity in something other than their former occupation.

Many Christians are struggling with unnecessary identity issues due to confusion concerning [who they are and their clear purpose]. Apathy soon inflicts any Christian who lacks positive convictions and proper knowledge of what their part is in the body of Christ and the world. This condition is brought on by to the absence of a clear biblical worldview and spiritual sense of direction coupled with the exclusion of the Holy Spirit and His assigned ministry from a great portion of the local churches in the United States and the Western World. The Apostle John exposed the major contributing factors for this condition.

He pointed out two distinct groups of people *operating* within the church; and both are clearly manifested today:

1. The children of God[1] [the redeemed]

2. The children of the devil [the unredeemed]

John contrasts the groups using Cain and Abel as examples:

- Abel came by faith and was accepted; while Cain tried to be saved by works, but was not accepted (see Genesis 4).

- Cain was a liar and a murderer, like the devil (see John 8:44). He murdered his brother and then lied to God about it.

- Genesis 3:15 states that Satan's seed (his unregenerate children) will oppose God's seed (His righteous seed).

- Cain worshiped at an altar – Satan's children (the unregenerate) know how to act religious.

- True love for God and His children is the test of our appreciation for God. At the new birth, the true child of God receives a *new nature* which changes our character traits (study Galatians 5:17-23).

- Additionally we receive the love of God and the Holy Spirit in our hearts (see Romans 5:5). With the true children of God, Christianity is a matter of the heart not the tongue as with the religious. The Pharisees are good examples of those who talk the talk, but don't walk the walk. We have the witness of the Spirit in our hearts that we are the children of God (see Romans 8:14-16).

Without the help of the Holy Spirit Christians individually and corporately are of little use to the kingdom of God on earth. The natural or the carnal minds used often in attempts to explain spiritual things have resulted in much heresy and theological confusion in the church. Many people through biblical and spiritual ignorance try to wash their hands of the Holy Spirit; just as Pilate *thought* he could do with Jesus.

This condition has left many local churches powerless, vulnerable and unable to influence the world around them. Satan seems to be using the spirit of Balaam as he used the prophet Balaam, himself in the Old Testament. When God blocked Balaam's attempt to curse Israel at the king's request, Balaam then suggested contamination through the women of Moab, a direct violation of God's moral law; which caused the death of thousands (see Numbers 31:16).

Today unable to abolish Christianity, Satan has flooded the country with many false gods, religions, secular philosophies such as evolution, secular humanism, multiculturalism and atheism, with the very purpose of contaminating Christianity; and very subtly causing widespread confusion, especially among the millennials and at the same time creating havoc and considerable collateral damage to traditional values, marriage and the family, early childhood education and training and corruption in all levels of government in our national society.

Satan has so organized his children in the local culture and church with the same mission, and he certainly has made inroads in those churches operating through parliamentary procedures and other policies; which they prize above biblical and spiritual truth. Satan's people specialize in knowing how to rally for their causes.

Today it's called "progressive Christianity" contaminate the people and the things of God by bringing them down to flesh level. God forbid! This is seen in the widening gulf between traditional Christian values and the contemporary moral values. Cohabitation, multi-marriages and multi-divorces and other sins are pulling many churches into the realm of Romans 1:21, and also like the Corinthians some are even patting themselves on the back for being so openly broad-minded! Many of them are sincere, but sincerely wrong! (See 1 Corinthians 5).

However the sad truth is these new so-called progressive [*relative*] Christians are subtly demanding of the church:

- "Coexistence"

- "A new tolerance"

- "Keep out of it"

- The abolishing of their true Christian convictions

- Excluding the Holy Spirit and His ministry

- Promoting an entertaining worship

- Promoting a gospel full of compromise

- This also places all of the church's services, ministries and activities mainly to each other within the four walls of the church building.

I pray this book will sound a wake-up call to America at large and our churches in particular. The present condition should be a major concern for every true child of God; and alert church leaders to fortify themselves and their people with the knowledge of God and Christ, the Holy Spirit and the truth of God's Word; which will enable them "to stand" during the present demonic onslaught on the church and culture in these last and evil days – very similar to the conditions faced by the early church, being revisited among Christian communities in the Middle East and parts of Africa today. Satan is turning up the heat on the children of God, "for he knows he has but a short time!" (see Revelation 12:12).

The mature Spirit-filled child of God must be fed up with the present-day contamination of the gospel, outrageous global persecutions, marketplace and cultural pressures on Christians everywhere [USA] today. But the clear and present danger is the lack of relevant attention to our millennials who through a lack of a biblically-taught worldview seem to not only love it, but insist that it is the "new progressive" way.

So if you look for the culture it's assimilated into the church and if you look for the church it is assimilated into the culture. This is not a time to be silent! Don't let the devil steal or force your biblical [witness of truth] from the church or cultural conversation!

– Jay R. Leach

Dynamic living

The last element of the Great Commissions given by our Lord to His disciples and activated for His Church throughout the ages is to "boldly stand" as His representatives and ministers of reconciliation to the "entire world." The Scripture reports that He said to them:

> "But you **shall receive power** when **the Holy Spirit** has come upon you, and you **shall be witnesses to Me** in Jerusalem, and in all Judea and Samaria, and to the end of the earth" (Acts 1:8). Emphasis added.

This power means supernatural ability to *witness* for Christ. Some writers conclude this verse applied to the apostles of the early church only, as being the recipients of this supernatural power. This has proven to be a hindrance and stumbling block to the spiritual growth of the church; this commitment includes every member. The Scripture notes 120 followers experienced the Holy Spirit in the Upper Room on Pentecost. Therefore the 120 received the power to witness. That Holy Ghost power is what enabled Peter to boldly confront thousands of Jews. His preaching was so effective that those who heard were "cut to the heart" *by the Holy Spirit* and they asked, "What shall we do?"(see Acts 2:37). This is the same Peter who cowardly denied even knowing Jesus – now he tells these powerful Jews what to do. Then Peter said to them,

> "Repent, and let every one of you be baptized in the name of Jesus Christ for the remission of sins; and you shall receive the gift of the Holy Spirit. For the promise is to you and to your children, and to all who are afar off, as many as the Lord our God will call" (see Acts 2:38-39).

From our Lord's promise, the power of the Holy Spirit is relevant and available to every child of God, not only for insight and witnessing, possibly on the scale of Peter on the Day of Pentecost; but also for holy living and other demonstrations of the supernatural power of God.

I am righteous (2 Corinthians 5:21)

Any person's preparation and concern with changing who they are can be accomplished only as a result of their repentance and receiving salvation through the finished work of Jesus Christ (study John 3:3; Romans 10:9-10; and 2 Corinthians 5:17).

Then heed the Apostle Peter's admonish to grow in grace and the knowledge of our Lord and Savior, Jesus Christ (see 2 Peter 1:2):

> *"As His divine power has given to us all things that pertain to life and godliness, through the knowledge of Him who called us by glory and virtue, by which He has given to us exceedingly great and precious promises, that through these <u>you may be partakers of the divine nature</u> ......"* (see 2 Peter 2-4). Emphasis added.

If not careful, at this point many young Christians will enter their Christian life trying to **do righteously** [in their own strength]. Here is the crucial *place in the salvation process!* The teacher or witness must clearly explain the fact that [under grace] you have been **made righteous or justified by God** (see 2 Corinthians 5:21).

Justification and righteousness are inseparably united in Scripture by the fact that the same word (*dikaios*, "righteous"; *dikaioo*, "to justify")[2] is used for both. The believing sinner is justified because Christ having borne his or her sins on the cross – *"has been made unto him [or her] righteousness"* (see 1 Corinthians 1:30). It very important also to know concerning justification:

- It originates in the grace of God (see Romans 3:24; Titus 3:4, 5).

- It is through the redemptive and propitiatory work of Christ, who has vindicated the law (see Romans 3:24, 25; 5:9).

- It is by faith, not works that we have done (Romans 3:28-30; 4:5; 5:1; Galatians 2:16; 3:8, 24).

- It may be defined as the judicial act of God whereby He justly declares righteous one who believes on Jesus Christ (v. 21).

- It is the Judge Himself who makes this declaration (see Romans 8:31-34).

Therefore, the person is justified, that is, "declared righteous," apart from doing what the law requires. Thus salvation is through **saving faith alone** (see Romans 4:23-25).

No matter what we do or think, we cannot earn our salvation. God alone saves, and His salvation is a free gift. No one can stand before God and boast of their good works. God is the only One who is righteous, and for that reason, He deserves our best of everything. In 1 Peter 2:24, Christ Himself says,

> "..... to Him who judges righteously; who Himself bore our sins in His own body on the tree, that we, having died to sins, might live for **righteousness** – by whose stripes you were healed.

The purpose of Christ's bearing our sins is that we might live godly lives to please Him. Thus, emphasizing His personal involvement in the act of paying the price for our sins. Each person must take responsibility for their own growth process. The differences made in the daily lives of the church's members manifest the children of God and the children of the devil.

It is my prayer that God will raise up an army of men and women wholly committed to Him, mature children of God, who prioritize:

- Making disciples,
- Baptizing them, and
- Teaching them all things as Christ, our Savior and Lord, has commanded.

We must be faithful to Christ and disciple others for Him beginning in our own homes, then going everywhere – to shake the gates of hell while passing on Christ and the life of godliness to the next generation. This is the kingdom agenda for the true children of God.

CHAPTER SUMMARY: CHAPTER 1

1. Those persons ages _____ to _____ are called Millennials.

2. There are two groups of people in the church _____ of _____ and _____ of the _____.

3. Abel   brought   his _____ by _____.

4. The love for God and His people is the test of our _____ of _____.

5. Without the Holy Spirit Christians individually and corporately are of little _____ to the _____ of _____ on earth.

6. The new so-called _____ Christians demand "_____" and "_____".

7. Christians should build themselves up in the _____ _____ _____ faith.

8. Justification originates in the _____ of God.

9. Christ took our sins that we might live _____ _____ to please Him.

10. The daily lives of church members manifest the _____ of _____ and the _____ of the _____.

CHAPTER 2

NONE BUT THE RIGHTEOUS

"For in the righteousness of God is revealed from faith to faith; as it is written, the just shall live by faith" (Romans 1:17).

Because of the misuse and in many cases lack of truth concerning *grace* in so many of our churches, we find little obvious difference between those who are in the church and those who are not. To the extent that this is true, represents serious identity flaws for Christianity, Christians and their churches alike.

A clear commitment to Jesus Christ involves the acceptance of purpose, and mission which *should* lead to action. Each child of God has his or her own unique personality, virtues, worldview, spiritual gift (s), and special place in God's plan in the body of Christ.

When considering the Christians' identity, some factors relate to what we are; and others to what we do. Being and doing combine to establish our identity and destiny [who we are and whose we are].

"God's interest is in what we are – before what we do."
– Jay R. Leach

Thus, it would seem that the home and church would be the places to begin and complete this formation respectively. The culture has so focused attention on working – that, we tend to ignore our being. Sadly, this is the case with too many local churches. And sharing the preoccupation with working, church leaders have all but lost sight of their responsibility as the spiritual trainers and developers for our spiritual formation, "being."

All members of Christ's Church should share spiritually in both the individual and corporate sense of righteousness. They are shaped by the shared unity, values and revealed biblical truth of the group so that distinct individual actions are in harmony with the absolute will of God.

What we are eventually is expressed through our character and then our work. Inconsistencies in either area will affect who we are, and your work will probably not survive or if continued be a source of drudgery rather than fulfillment. Many functions once carried out by the church as their responsibilities, biblically due to their spiritual nature are gradually being usurped by the domains of secular government and private agencies.

Therefore the churches' role in helping people comes to grips with the fact that spiritual problems require biblical solutions which often conflict with the secular community. As a result these problems are often ignored and many times spiral out of control once the individual has been rationalized or medicalized through attempts by secular agencies to treat symptoms rather than the cause.

Adding fuel to the fire is the humanistic watchword, *"whatever-it-seems-is-the-ONLY-way-to-be!"* This hopeless statement has indoctrinated millions of Americans, generation after generation through the public school systems, media and the government. How can the church rely on secularists and atheists who do not believe in God and the supernatural to deal with spiritual problems? Yet, I'm sure many demonically influenced secular leaders are laughing at many local churches who try to pack all of their work into one or two hours on Sunday. In fact many are hiring their own secular priests to fill the void. Actually, the Spirit is to assign and work specific in on-going cases through the spiritually-mature children of God in the body of Christ!

The problem goes even deeper. The most important question concerns the difference when the church relies on the spiritual truths of God's Word versus the secular behavioral modification or other worldly strategies that cannot reach deep enough to treat the actual cause. The fundamental issue is does the church make a difference? Even more to the point, does that relationship with God through Jesus Christ, which is the basis of church membership, make a difference in the lives of those believers who are in fellowship with the church? The mandate remains, "make disciples and teach them to do all ..." (Matthew 28:19-20).

Much of what is written about the church today speaks from a culturally influenced point of view rather than a biblically based view. And too much of it is focused on being done within the church's four walls rather than among the people and communities outside. Notice the programmatic-type issues below:

- How to be a better you.
- How to attract and keep new people.
- How to have a successful building fund-raising campaign.
- How to build a successful Sunday school.
- How to build a successful recreation program for our youth.
- How to build our young people for tomorrow's church, meanwhile just wait your turn.

Little is written to help the Christian with the identity problem mentioned earlier in chapter one; which accounts for the majority of the problems of ordinary people in the pews. These are people from the marketplace professionals, common laborers even some unemployed, at home spouses, and others who really want to honor God in their work and influence friends and other acquaintances for Christ. This group represents a potential army of witnesses for the kingdom of God.

Satan's hierarchy operates on money

I think we underestimate Satan, and I'm sure he is pleased! He has organized his demons into legions. Likewise he is the prince of this world's [systems]. He assigns his unregenerate children to operate *behind* the systems called worlds i.e. the world of sports, the world of politics, the world of finances, the world of fitness, the world of services, the world of education, world of medicine even the world of religion. These systems are the brain children of men many whom are under demonic influence.

Unless a person is under godly influence, "others" is probably a foreign term with little or no meaning to them. Money is their motivator and people are employed only to help them get more of it.

The rich person hires employees to make money for them; however the system is not designed to make the employees rich, otherwise who would do the work. Over indulgence in *any* world system will consume you. Listen to a few worldly examples:

- In the social system, a woman is told you can get a relief check, but not until your husband is out of the house!

- In another a preacher using sports illustrations in sermons that appeal mostly to the men present not considering women and children present.

- Thinking money is the answer to all of your worldly problems. If you listen to the world and follow their lead – the systems are designed to operate with man as the head. Therefore, God, Christ and the children of God in many cases have no place.

- The systems are designed to convince you that you don't need God or Christ to survive, just get side jobs, in fact if you really want the world's respect work two or three jobs. Listen to the world, "that's just the way it is!" The world's greatest fear is running out of money.
  After all, money literally makes the world go around!

Heaven's monarchy operates on grace through faith

This book is about helping you, that is, the true child of God to find your purpose and help equip you "to be" the person through whom God can supernaturally get to the root of the world's spiritual problems [sin] in those people in your area of influence and "by faith" through the Spirit and the power of the Gospel render them set free from sin and healed. Using the approach of "what you are" [as determined by your righteousness and obedience] comes before "what you do"[your works], enables you to be a capable instrument of righteousness who ministers and helps io equip others in their salvation experience, spiritual growth in "the faith" and their calling.

Much of our ministering to others should be concerned with insuring that the believers are properly taught the truth of God's Word. This may be by "one on one" or through other means in that church's concept of ministry. For example: It is imperative that we counter their (supposed) need of things that they have been conditioned through cultural indoctrination to believe are only accessible through hard-earned cash. But at the same time many are taught; but refuse to grasp the fact that heaven's currency is grace through faith in God and His promises.

Satan, through a secular cultural indoctrination has most people convinced that the husband [breadwinner] and the wife [mother] in the home raising godly children, though it is the biblical concept, are considered foolish, outdated and cruel. Society has ruled that she should be free to pursue her own stuff, and therefore, it's a cultural norm for her to have full-time employment; in fact even a second job if needed [to acquire more stuff] is not out of the question today!

Materialism has been one of the main culprits against biblical marriage and the family; the Christian church and true Christian spirituality. With the popularity of cremations and funerals being held within the funeral home's facility, we have a generation of parents raising a generation of children who have never been inside a church building. Biblical ignorance being what it is today, the only faith many know is the common faith in things like the brakes on the car or to trust the chair will hold them up.

Atheistic faith and spirituality based on relativity have made inroads in the church today. In the haste of busyness, traditional

Christian trust practices are subtly being omitted. I have listed a few below:

- Seeking the will of God.
- Seeking the unity of the church in mission.
- Preparing for a decision by listening to God in prayer.
- Waiting for the anointing of the Holy Spirit.

These decisions are increasingly rare and foreign to the leadership in many local churches today. The prevailing trends in the church today is to rely so heavily on preprogrammed flow charts, and packaged presentations that little reliance if any is upon the Lord.

CHAPTER SUMMARY: CHAPTER 2

1. Those persons ages 11-34 are known a _____.

2. Many of the local churches are struggling with who they are because they lack a viable world_____.

3. According to this writer, John points out two groups in the church _____ and _____.

4. Abel moved _____ with his offering.

5. _____ is the test of our appreciation for new God.

6. At the new birth the child of God receives a new _____.

7. Christianity is a matter of the _____ and not the _____.

8. When Satan could not abolish Christianity to this day he tries to _____ it.

9. Justification originates in the _____ of God.

10. The differences made in the _____ _____ of the churches' members manifest the true and false.

CHAPTER 3

THE ASSESSMENT

"Do not withhold good from those to whom it is due,
when it is in the power of your hand to do so"
(Proverbs 3:27).

The church in the twenty-first century is experiencing an unprecedented crisis. In some locations the exodus from the church is considerably larger than growth in new members. Barna tracking research has determined several conclusions concerning people who possess a *biblical worldview*:

1. They are more stable.
2. They believe that absolute moral truth exists.
3. They believe the source of moral truth is the Bible.
4. They believe that Satan is a living being.[3]

Even with all of the available research and other resources, many born again Christians hold a confusing and contradictory set of Christian beliefs that are allowed to go on unchecked by the leaders and teachers of their churches. I remember as a child we were taught

100 reasons why we were Baptists, We learned Bible verses and much more but being a good Baptist meant following traditional church customs, policies, and procedures seemed to be the top priority – in many cases over Scriptural truth.

In the early 70's research revealed that African American adults generally emerged as the ethnic segment most deeply committed to the Christian faith – today that status has changed significantly to less than either whites or Hispanics to have a biblical worldview. As an African American this picture is very hurtful. When many of us left home it was the influence that drove many of us in the language of our parents, "to make something of ourselves" – and "don't forget to always give God the glory!" Praise God for godly parents!

Looking at the overall problem and what it is doing to the church of Jesus Christ, all of the groups are less than favorable and continuing to fall. Proportionately the number of young people in our church training ministries is a shamefully small percentage of those living in the surrounding communities. One of the big hindrances today stems from:

- The idea that evangelism is outdated and no longer needed
- Self-centered Christians
- Spiritual and biblical ignorance
- Lack of a personal relationship with the Lord
- Lack of commitment to the Great Commission
- Lack of Church teaching and training.
- Loss of interest, and the list goes on and on

Other Observations

One of the chief missions of the church in this hour is its own restoration; through a fuller use of the entire membership in the ministry and missions of the church. We all know and can feel what's coming in this country. O' but what a privilege it is to stand for Jesus Christ when it means something. The church must vigorously engage all age groups in the pursuit of a biblical worldview that they may:

- Possess radically different views on morality than the atheistic/ humanistic views promoted by the world, the flesh, and the devil in the culture today.

- Hold divergent biblical beliefs without compromise [there is no wiggle room].

- Demonstrate different lifestyle choices as we are led by the Holy Spirit and the Word.

The greatest gain in converts is not where the most money is raised, but where the most Christians are at work personally witnessing and winning their neighbors for Christ.

The importance of right thinking

Because our minds are the conduits that God uses through our "born again" spirits and new natures to influence the world around us; it is imperative for us to understand that negative thinking can destroy our best efforts for spiritual growth in the kingdom of God. *"As a man thinks in his heart, so is he"* [or she] (Proverbs 23:7).

Unfortunately, a great deal of church research today indicates that many pastors who consider themselves spokespersons for God are misleading their congregations by not addressing critical cultural issues of the day nor preaching and teaching the biblical truth concerning these matters. If the pastors and teachers do not heed the necessity of such an important priority, the solidity of the church's foundational purposes will be questionable and compromise will fill the gaps.

> *"And be not conformed to this world, but be transformed by the renewing of your mind, that you may prove what is that good and acceptable and perfect will of God" (Romans 12:2).*

Based on God's mercy, Paul admonishes all believers to present their bodies a living sacrifice, meaning they should be obedient and use their bodies to serve the Lord. This refers to all parts of the body such as the hands and the mouth are not to be used as a means of sinning. For example: Do not use your hands to steal or your mouth to lie. We are to use our individual body parts as instruments of righteousness.

The kingdom agenda requires a total commitment to God. He admonishes that we all be transformed through the renewing of our minds, in order to know the acceptable and perfect will of God. This commitment carries us far beyond our initial acceptance of Christ as our personal Savior. This requires separation [transformation] unto God.

Spiritual Transformation

Spiritual transformation or sanctification begins in our spirit when we are born again; with a new nature, changed mind and heart.

> *"Therefore, if anyone is in Christ, he [or she] is a new creation; olf things have passed away; behold all things have become new"* (see 2 Corinthians 5:17).

Therefore indicates that the verse above is a conclusion drawn from the previous one. A mind dedicated to the world and its concerns as is so prevalent in our culture and many churches today produces a life tossed to and fro [utter confusion]. But a spiritual mind dedicated to the guidance of the Holy Spirit and the truth of God's Word produces a life that can stand the tests of faithfulness to God, Christ and the Church. It is imperative that we get a right understanding for the tests of our faith are sure to come in these evil days:

Figure #1	Figure #2
WRONG	RIGHT
ORDER BEFORE SALVATION	ORDER AFTER SALVATION
(natural man)	(spiritual man)
SOUL [FLESH]	SPIRIT [QUICKENED]
BODY	soul [flesh]
spirit [DEAD]	body

We can resist the temptations of our culture by meditating on God's Word and allowing the Holy Spirit to guide and shape our thoughts and behaviors based on truth:

- Prior to being "born again" the whole person is ruled or controlled by their sinful nature through his or her SOUL also called the FLESH which comprises their [mind, affections (feelings), and will]. See figure #1 above.

- When we are born again[*regeneration*] the Holy Spirit quickens or brings to life our spirit [which was dead due to sin] and we partake of God's divine nature; which changes our mind and inner being through the love of God and the Holy Spirit which is given to us (see Romans 5:5).

- We are now in proper alignment with God's order; so our SPIRIT made righteous, takes its rightfully *justified* place, in control and begins to be led of the Holy Spirit, this person is in the process of separation [*transformation*] to present to God your most prized possession [your body], a living sacrifice, holy, and acceptable to God which is your reasonable service." See figure #2 above.

- The Holy Spirit affects a definite change to begin working immediately from our inside to the outside [study 2 Corinthians 5:17], as we are a new creation by the incorruptible Seed. Through the imparted love of God, and divine nature; the Holy Spirit leads and guides us into all truth (study John 16:13):

  1. He produces and develops the fruit of the Spirit in us (study thoroughly Galatians 5:22-23).

     This fruit developed in us are Christlike-character qualities which the Holy Spirit grows in us as He molds us into the image of God's Son.

2. He gives and develops a spiritual gift (s) within us equipping us for the Lord's service (study carefully 1 Corinthians 12-14).

The reward for finding and putting into practice your spiritual gift or gifts is the personal blessing of knowing that you are biblically in the will of God (carefully study Romans 12:1-6).

The Apostle Peter wrote, "As each has received a gift, employ it for one another, as good stewards of God's varied grace" (1 Peter 4:10). Again, a spiritual gift is a special anointing that God gives to each true child of God. They are given to function around His eternal objectives. Clearly these gifts of the Holy Spirit are not given to entertain, excite the congregation, or to promote individuals and their ministries.

Many desire to move in the Spiritual gifts primarily to be seen of men. It is God's purpose and desire "that all men be saved and come into the knowledge of the truth" (see 1Timothy 2:4). The *gifts* from 1 Corinthians 12:7-11, listed below should be operating in every local church:

Five speaking gifts (v. 7)

- Prophecy
- Teaching
- Encouragement
- The word of wisdom
- The word of knowledge

Seven service gifts (v. 8)

- Helps
- Mercy
- Faith
- Discernment of spirits
- Leadership
- Managing
- Giving

The church, an organism, is Christ's unified body under the headship of Christ, but the members [like the members of a human body [i.e. an "arm" or "leg"] have different functions, all for the purpose of spiritually edifying – building up all the members in the church, the body.

The gifts of the Spirit always bear witness to the truth of the Gospel. Therefore the manifestation of the Spirit and the Word working in tandem produces the following:

1. A seed is planted in the heart and
2. A conversion takes place

Paul explains, *"But if all prophesy, and an unbeliever or uninformed person comes in, he is convinced by all, he is convicted by all. And thus the secrets of his heart are revealed; and so, falling down on his face, he will worship God and report that God is fully among you"* (1 Corinthians 14:24-25).

This means all of God's children publically proclaim the Word of God. The power is in the Word not us:

- We are conformed to Christ's image gradually as we spend time in intimate fellowship with Him (see 2 Corinthians 3:18).

- We are filled with the Spirit (Ephesians 5:18).

The effect on unbelievers would be amazingly powerful, the gospel would be honored, and souls would be converted to worship God.

Transformed for the Lord's service

Now justified (righteous), transformed (separated unto God), and consecrated (in the Lord's service); we are *not* to be conformed [shaped] by the world's systems. Jesus said,

> *"I have given them your word; and the world has hated them because **they are not of this world, just as I am not of the world"*** (John 17:14). Emphasis added throughout.

24

The present world-systems have been in the ethically bad-sense of the word highly influenced by Satan. Unless interrupted by God-consciousness through the power of the Gospel, a person's thinking and living will automatically be shaped by these satanically arranged world systems. For example, before we were saved the parents, church, media, culture, school, siblings, teachers, friends, and the world around us had a profound influence in conforming or shaping the way we thought, [our worldview], habits, and even our way of living our lives.

Satan, the prince of this world has organized the world of **unbelieving humankind [his children]** upon the cosmic principles of:

- Force
- Greed
- Selfishness
- Ambition and
- Pleasure

If we do not let God complete the cleansing begun in the "new birth," we may become pastors, teachers or other Christian workers, but hear this —unless you are completely delivered from Satan's **sinful principles and concepts,** believe me when you least expect it, they will come back to haunt you. Don't under estimate Satan's manipulative power. You've heard it said, and it's true – he will nurture that speck of sin in you, and then spring it when it is to his advantage. Emphasis added.

Remember, Satan is not your friend and he does not love you! So what he does will be aimed at destruction of your reputation as God's child, God's people, your family and friends – lowly or lofty your fall will cause great harm to the kingdom of God, especially to those just starting out in the faith.

"You are probably thinking that will never happen to me!" Unless you are fully submitted and fully committed through a right and loving relationship with God in Christ; and allow His cleansing through the Word by the Holy Spirit – watch out!

No matter what your position – if you are knowledgeable of sin in you, and you don't repent and forsake it, but let it continue for whatever reason, then you are likely a candidate! Satan himself will be the first one to throw up in your face, "you knew better!" You know who I am and what I am about but! ....!"

I read an illustration some time ago about a farmer's helper doing the early spring plowing; he plowed up a frozen poisonous snake. He placed the snake within his clothing next to his warm chest to thaw it out. Soon the old snakes head emerged with his flickering tongue and bite him right between the eyes. As the man lay dying, he asked the snake why he bit him after all he had done for him! His reply, "I'm a snake ain't I?"

A friend of ours was picking up pine cones and twigs in her backyard after a summer storm had passed through, she reached for a stick; which moved away, just in the nick of time – it was a copperhead (a poison viper snake). Don't play with snakes! God has given His children "the truth," the Holy Bible hear what He has warned about our handling of it:

> *"For I testify to everyone who hears the words of the prophecy of this book: If anyone adds to these things, God will add to him the plagues that are written in this book; and if anyone takes away from the words of the book of this prophecy, God shall take away his part from the Book of Life, from the holy city, and from the things which are written in this book"* (Revelation 22:18-19).

Jesus commissioned John to write this prophecy, but He is the Author. These are not the first such warnings (see Deuteronomy 4:2; 12:32; Proverbs 30:6; Jeremiah 26:2). Anyone who tampers *with the truth* by attempting to:

- Falsify
- Mitigate
- Alter
- Misinterpret it

Those who do so will incur the judgments described in these verses. Jesus offers extended testimony on the authority and finality of the prophecy: The Holy Spirit, our Helper, whom Jesus promised from the Father is here and in us to:

- lead us,
- teach us,
- and reveal to us the truth of God's Word (see John 26).

Sin is a principle

As stated earlier, methods change, but principles stay the same. If principles are changed it can only happen outside the natural realm, so that means if the sin principle you are harboring is to be changed only God can do it. Research shows that the sin principle is operating full speed ahead in the local churches in many cases at the same level as in the world outside. Why?

- First the "flesh" convinces you that you can't help it.

- Second, the humanistic/ atheistic charged culture says, "That's just the way it is."

- Turn to God – He is your only hope! (Supernatural transformation).

Transformation brings with it a total change in your thinking to a biblical view of the world, godly character, attitudes, and virtues. Now as children of God your worldview is being shaped through your personal relationship with Christ and through obeying the Holy Spirit and the truths of God's Word. God knows our tendencies toward trying to live holy in the flesh (prayerfully study Romans7-8); which is overcome only by our constantly walking according to the Spirit:

God made it clear in His Word that this was never His will for us. His Word says,

> *"There is therefore now no condemnation to those who are in Christ Jesus, who do not walk according to the flesh, but according to the Spirit"* (Romans 8:1).

> *"But you shall receive power when the Holy Spirit has come upon you; and you shall be witnesses to Me in Jerusalem, and in all Judea and Samaria, and to the end of the earth"* (Acts 1:8).

Walking according to the Spirit is the proper response to the powerful gospel of Christ that we heard and received in our hearts. According to Paul our motivation to pursue transformation is found in the mercies of God. We do it out of a sense of appreciation for what the Lord has done for us. One great theologian summed it up,

> "If Jesus Christ is God and died for me,
> then no sacrifice
> can be too great for me
> to make for Him!"

"As a man thinks in his heart, so is he (Proverbs 23:7)."

Remember, a renewed mind requires a change of worldview; which can be achieved only through a right relationship with Christ. Notice Matthew 6:33 admonishes each of us:

> *"But seek first the kingdom of God and His righteousness, and all these things shall be added to you."*

As I stated in an earlier section, many sincere followers of Christ are confused and through cultural influences they follow a deceptive secular humanistic worldview. The biblical worldview gets contaminated as the secular world bombards us constantly from television, films, music, newspapers, magazines, books and academia.

In his book, *Understanding the Times,* author David Noebel states that, "a biblical worldview is based on the infallible Word of God.

When you believe the Bible is entirely true, then you allow it to be the foundation of everything you say and do."

Yet, so many are determined to continue their downward spiral and would rather suffer along with the world than turn fully to God. The total reality of this worldly view among many so-called "relative" Christians results in broken marriages, broken off springs and families, cohabitation, no respect for life, sexual perversions, all culminating in wasted lives and ineffective witness. With each passing day the culture's laws and norms try to slither their way into the church orchestrated by none other than Satan's children.

Many church members even some who love the Lord are deceived because of spiritual and biblical ignorance enhanced through a smorgasbord of second and third-handed time spun irreligious beliefs and opinions. There are many who are sincere in their thinking, but sincerely wrong!

Again we hear the humanistic/ atheistic theme, **"what-ever-it-seems-is-the-ONLY-way-to-be!"** Our children are being indoctrinated with that [hopeless] theme daily through the atheistic/ humanistic education presented and rehearsed daily in the public school systems across this nation. We see where this is leading; just catch any newscast.

Yet we refuse to connect the dots. So each day we are introduced to more and more diabolical spirits in specific places and some people of influence. There are more bolder waves of crime and mayhem as our public officials at all levels deny and try to remove the only true answer, Jesus Christ, from the public square, by continuing to put their trust in humanity's so-called technological advances, science and "relative" reason. This is Adam and Eve's sin [from the tree of the knowledge of good and evil, repackaged (see Genesis 2:8-10).

The Scripture says,

> *"Whose minds, the god of this age has blinded, who do not believe, lest the light of the gospel of the glory of Christ, who is the image of God, should shine on them"* (see 2 Corinthians 4:4).

Fleshly thoughts, ideas, speculations, reasoning, philosophies, and false religions are ideological *strongholds* in which people barricade themselves against God, His Son, His children and the gospel. For the wisdom of this world is foolishness with God.

For it is written,

> *"He catches the wise in their own craftiness,"* and again, *"The Lord knows the thoughts of the wise, that they are futile"* (see 1 Corinthians 3:20).

The true kind of transformation and restoration of your mind occurs only as the Holy Spirit changes your thinking. Again notice in Romans 12:2 that the perfect will of God is only reached as we renew our minds. Paul says in Colossians 3:1-5, 9, and 10:

> *"If then you were raised with Christ,*
> *seek those things which are above,*
> *where Christ is,*
> *sitting at the right hand of God.*
>
> *Set your mind on things above,*
> *not on things on the earth.*
>
> *For you died,*
> *and your life is hidden with Christ*
> *in God.*
>
> *When Christ who is our life appears,*
> *then you also will appear*
> *with Him in glory.*
>
> *Therefore put to death your members*
> *which are on the earth: fornication,*
> *uncleanness, passion, evil*
> *desires, and covetousness*
> *which is idolatry.*
> *Do not lie to one another,*

Since you have put off
the old man with his deeds,

And have put on the new man
who is renewed in knowledge
according to the image of Him
who created Him.

The divine exchange is putting off the old man, and putting on the new man which is renewed in the knowledge of God. We give up the old way [nature], and receive a whole new [nature] way of living. We leave the kingdom of the devil, and enter into the kingdom of God's dear Son. We exchange our old way of thinking and acting for a new way. Paul says this new man is recreated according to the image of Christ. In Romans 8:29 he says:

> *"For whom He foreknew, He also predestined to be conformed to the image of His Son, that He might be the firstborn among many brethren."*

As we exchange our ways for His, we begin to experience this abundant life that Paul is talking about. We are no longer controlled by the thoughts, attitudes, desires and actions of the world. We are no longer moved by the world, the flesh and the devil. We rise up to new controlling sources – the Spirit and Word of God. Isaiah 55:7-9 says,

> *"Let the wicked forsake his ways, and the unrighteous man his thoughts; let him [or her] return to the Lord, and He will have mercy on him; and to our God, for He will abundantly pardon. For My thoughts are not your thoughts, nor are your ways My ways," says the Lord." For as the heavens are higher than the earth, so are My ways higher than your ways, and My thoughts than your thoughts."*

In this passage the Spirit is exhorting us to give up our old thoughts and ways to exchange them for Christ's higher level of life.

Remember, to have God's ways, we must have His thoughts. Let us make the exchange and rise up to this higher life:

- We give up our low life – and receive His higher life.

- We give up death – and receive His life.

- We give up sin – and receive His righteousness.

- We give up sickness – and receive His healing.

- We give up poverty – and receive His prosperity.

- We give up what we have in the natural realm – and receive what is His in the spiritual realm.

> Jesus makes it clear, *"He who finds his life will lose it, and he who loses his life for My sake will find it"* (Matthew 10:39).

Only for those who come to Christ with self-denouncing faith, will there be true and eternal life. As Christ's body and Spirit-led representatives in the world, we are not authorized to make people think in anyway or form that His call for total commitment has been rescinded or modified in any way. As your spiritual life progresses, you will experience your thought life being changed from Christlessness to Christlikeness. The Scripture requires,

> For *"who has known the mind the mind of the Lord that he may instruct him? 'But we have the mind of Christ"* (see 1 Corinthians 2:16).

In 2 Corinthians 3:14-15, Paul pictures the fact that Moses communicated the glory of the Old Covenant with a certain obscurity. He expounds, that the people of Moses' day did not grasp the glory of it because of the veil of unbelief; and the veil was still there to those who trusted in it as a means of salvation in Paul's day.

The veil of ignorance hides the meaning of the Old Covenant to the hard hearted today. Without Christ the Old Testament is without understanding. However, the veil is removed when a person comes to Christ, and his or her perception is no longer impaired. The believers are able to see the glory of God revealed in Christ Jesus. In John 1:14 we read,

> *"And the Word became flesh and dwelt among us, and we beheld His glory, the glory as of the only begotten of the Father, full of grace and truth."*

In the New Testament, God chose to dwell among His people in a much more personal way, through becoming a man. Though His glory was veiled in human flesh, glimpses of His glory exist in the gospels of His divine majesty. The disciples saw His glory on the Mount of Transfiguration (see Matthew 17:1-8). His glory, however, was not only physical but also spiritual. They saw Him display the attributes or characteristics of God.

A few are listed below:

- Grace
- Goodness
- Mercy
- Wisdom
- Truth

These attributes of God's glory emphasizes the goodness of God's character, especially in relationship to salvation; as Jesus tabernacled among humanity in the New Testament era:

> *"For this reason we also, since the day we heard it, do not cease to pray for you, and to ask that you may be filled with the knowledge of His will in all wisdom and spiritual understanding; that you may walk worthy of the Lord, fully pleasing Him, being fruitful in every good work and increasing in the knowledge of God"* (Colossians 1:9-10; also study 14:14, 15, 19 and Luke 24:45).

33

True children of God are allowed by the Spirit and the Word, to know the thoughts of our Lord. That comes with full commitment to the higher life in Christ. Have you sold out, abandoned self and gone for it?

STUDY SUMMARY: CHAPTER 3

1. Our _____ are the conduits that God uses to _____ the world through us.

2. _____ thinking can destroy our best efforts for spiritual _____.

3. Explain in the <u>space below</u> what Paul meant by "present your body" a living sacrifice:

4. Spiritual transformation begins in our _____ when we are _____.

5. God's order of our being is _____ _____ and _____.

6. In regeneration the soul has to relent to the _____.

7. Numerous people desire to move into their _____ gift to the _____ of men.

8. The Spirit and the Word working in tandem manifests the _____ of _____.

9. Walking according to the Spirit is the proper response to the powerful _____ of Christ.

10. In the <u>space below</u> explain the requirements for us to know the perfect will of God:

CHAPTER 4

LOST AND FOUND

"Who has declared from the beginning,
that we may know?
And former times, that we may say,' He is righteous'?
Surely there is one who shows,
Surely there is no one who declares,
Surely there is no one who hears your words"
(Isaiah 41:26).

In many of the larger malls and businesses, we can find a section usually in the customer service department called lost and found. Sometimes when children get unattached from their parents and wander off, eventually after much searching the parent hear over the building's public address system a voice reporting that a little lost child fitting the description of your little one has been brought to the lost and found section. "Please come and get your child!" Similarly God has sent Jesus for His lost children.

As we saw in the last chapter, in creation God created man with a spirit, a soul comprising (a mind, affections, freewill), and a body giving humanity the ability to make choices. God created man [Adam] perfect and placed him in a perfect environment, the Garden of Eden. God Himself cared for him and met his every need. He gave him a wife [Eve]. Their total inward focus was toward God and their perfect fellowship with Him.

God gave Adam dominion [rule] over His creation, even to the naming of the various animals. He had everything:

- a perfect wife
- a perfect home
- a perfect employment [king with a little "k" of course]

While sin was not in them, the propensity to sin was possible through their freewill; which up to this point was in God's will. The test of that freewill came to light when God pointed out a tree in the center of the Garden of Eden called the "tree of the knowledge of good and evil" which was the only tree in the garden forbidden to them. This gave Adam and Eve access to another tree in the Garden, the "tree of life."

In a sense Adam was limited as he could not decide for himself on moral issues. Judgment of right and wrong did not reside in him, but in God; so when faced with any question he had to refer it to God. Thus, his life was totally dependent upon God.

Another presence

Soon Adam and Eve would meet another presence in the garden a fallen angel, who was created perfect, and beautiful with music in his wings named Satan. Prior to his fall, Satan was Lucifer, "son of the morning" assigned duties in the very presence of God in heaven. Lifted up in pride he desired the very seat of His Creator, God [thus the original sin].

God put him out, but he carried with him a third of the angels which had fallen under his influence. His new abode became the air between heaven and earth where he organized his fallen angels, now demons into hierarchical styled legions. Though banished from heaven, and with a name change from Lucifer to Satan and the devil, he realized his crushed dreams of taking God's throne; and turned his attention to the destruction of God's creation and its highest point, humanity.

Adam and Eve had the perfect relationship with God walking and talking with Him in the cool of the evening, Satan stirred up pride within Eve by approaching her instead of Adam. His reversal of roles deceived her knowing that God had given dominion to Adam, not Eve. He began a conversation and led her to believe God was cheating or holding out on them. As if to say, He doesn't want you to know that you will become as gods if you eat of the tree of the knowledge of good and evil. She took the bait and ate, then gave to Adam who also ate. In so doing they became independent and without the life of God. This act of disobedience cost them their lives (Genesis 3:6).

If Adam and Eve had chosen "the tree of life" they would have partaken of the life of God. Thus, they would have become sons of God, as their lives are derived from God. The result would have been the union of God's life with man, *a new creation,* having the life of God in them and living in total dependence upon God for that life. This point will be expanded in a later chapter.

Remember, God said, "You will surely die" (see Genesis 2:17). Though Adam and Eve did not instantly die – they died! They died a [spiritual death, [alienation from God]. Their innocence noted in Genesis 2:25 had been replaced by nakedness, guilt and shame; and conscious [to know right from wrong]; now they could make decisions independent of God. Notice how they used this newly acquired power – they tried to cover through their own efforts with fig leaves.

Undoubtedly their decision to take care of their problem themselves was the results of relying on their conscious to distinguish between good and evil through their newly acquired capacity to see and know evil.

Where are you?

God came along just as He did in time past walking in some visible form probably Shekinah light as He later appeared in (see Exodus 33:1823; 34:5-8, 29; 40:34-38). He did not come in fury, but tones of goodness and kindness. What a mighty God we serve!

God was not expressing ignorance of where Adam and Eve were when He asked the question; but the question gave Adam, to whom

He had given dominion, a chance to explain why they were hiding and where they were hiding. Notice God addressed Adam, the head:

- shame
- remorse
- confusion
- guilt
- fear

All the above led to this evasive behavior. However, there was no place to hide, there never is or ever will be (see 3:8-10). While many may have problems with it, God set the order of the home He sat the husband as the head of the wife.

Any other arrangement is out of order – to choose any other way has to be out of God's will. Domineering wives and wimpy husbands are not exceptions. The battle of the sexes is not Christian and neither is the woman trying to usurp the man's power.

We can take a lesson from the psalmist David who expresses his awe that God knew him, even to the minutest detail. God has perfect knowledge of every person.

I will emphasize the point through an *Interlude* with Psalm 139:1-12:

*O Lord, You have searched me and
known me.
You know my sitting down and my
rising up;
You understand my thought afar off.
You comprehend my path and my
lying down,
And are acquainted with all my ways.
For there is not a word on my tongue,
But behold, O Lord, You know it
altogether.
You have hedged me behind and
before,
And laid Your hand upon me.
Such knowledge is too wonderful for;*

me;
It is high, I cannot attain it.
Where can I go from Your Spirit?
Or where can I flee from Your
presence?
If I ascend into heaven, You are there;
If I make my bed in hell, behold, You
are there.
If I take the wings of the morning,
And dwell in the uttermost parts of
the sea,
Even there Your hand shall lead me,
And Your right hand shall hold me.
If I say, "Surely the darkness shall
fall on me,"
Even the night shall be light about
me;
Indeed, the darkness shall not hide
from You,
But the night shines as the day;
The darkness and the light are both
alike to You.

For You formed my inward parts;
You covered me in my mother's
womb.
I will praise you for I am fearfully
And wonderfully made;
Marvelous are Your works,
And that my soul knows very well.
My frame was not hidden from You,
When I was made in secret,
And skillfully wrought in the lowest
parts of the earth.
Your eyes saw my substance, being
yet unformed.

God was always watching over David and thus it was impossible to do anything over which God is not a spectator. God does not change as it was with Adam and David, so shall it be with every child of God.

Back to Eden

God immediately set His plan of redemption into motion. The Scripture says,

> *"For Adam and his wife the Lord God made tunics of skin and clothed them"* (Genesis 3:21).

This act of mercy was a shadow of the reality that God would someday *kill a substitute to redeem sinners.* God did not curse Adam and Eve, but after He cursed the physical serpent to life on its belly eating the dust of the earth – He cursed the spiritual serpent, Satan. So the Lord God said to the serpent,

> *"And I will put enmity*
> *Between you and the woman,*
> *And between your seed and her*
> *Seed;*
> *He shall bruise your head,*
> *And you shall bruise His heel"*
> *(Genesis 3:15).*

This *"first gospel"* is a clear picture of the struggle and its outcome between *"your seed"* (Satan and unbelievers, called the devil's children in John 8:44) and *"her Seed"* (Christ, a descendent of Eve and those in Him). This enmity and warfare began in the Garden in the midst of the curse passage *[a promise and hope]* – the woman's offspring called "He" is Christ, who will one day defeat the serpent, Satan. Notice, he could only "bruise" Christ's heel (cause Him to suffer), while Christ will bruise Satan's head (destroy him with a fatal blow).

If Satan could do away with the first eleven chapters of the Book of Genesis, the rest of the Bible would be useless! But praise God – it is not within his power to do so!

True children of God can rejoice recognizing the fact that they will participate with their Savior in the crushing of Satan, because of His *finished work on the cross,* they are also of the woman's seed.

Her Seed – The Man, Jesus Christ

Jesus Christ was not only divine. He was also human. He was born of a woman, came under the law, and took upon Himself our very nature. In His deity, Jesus could not fully atone for the sins of the world. The sacrifice must also have the human element in it. Therefore, in dying for our sins, Christ had to die as a man. Prior to His death – He suffered in man's flesh.

> *"For indeed He does not give aid to angels, but He does give aid to the seed of Abraham. Therefore, in all things He had to be made like His brethren, that He might be a merciful and faithful High Priest in things pertaining to God, to make propitiation for the sins of the people. For in that He Himself has suffered, being tempted; He is able to aid those who are tempted"* (Hebrews 2:16-18).

His death and burial in the tomb had to be in the flesh, so that there would be assurance of a resurrection from the dead for all those who should believe on Him. The Apostle Paul admonishes:

> *"For if the dead do not rise then Christ is not risen. And if Christ is not risen, your faith is futile; you are still in your sins! Then also those who have fallen asleep in Christ have perished. If in this life only we have hope in Christ, we are of all men the most pitiable"* (1 Corinthians 15:16-23).

Christ's virgin birth is so beautifully set in the angel Gabriel's announcement to Mary. And the angel said to her,

> *"The Holy Spirit will come upon you, and the power of the Highest will overshadow you; therefore, also, that Holy One who is to be born will be called the Son of God"* (Luke 1:26-35).

Here then was real humanity. It was not the nature of angels that He assumed, but that of Abraham. He was, "in all things made like unto His brethren."

- He became one of them.

- He was subject to temptation.

- He knew the pain of suffering.

- He was not a stranger to the common problems of humankind.

For we do not have a High Priest who cannot sympathize with our weaknesses, but was in all points tempted as we are, yet without sin (Hebrews 4:15).

- In order to understand the weakness of human nature, He had to experience it.

- In order for Him to be sympathetic with men in their trials, He also had to be tried.

- He must experience hunger, weariness, disappointment, sorrow, and persecution.

- He must tread the same paths, live under the same circumstances, and die the same death.

When the Lord arose from the grave and ascended again to sit at the right hand of God, He went as a man – there to represent the human race as our older Brother, Advocate, and High Priest.

Death in Adam – Life in Christ

> *"Therefore, just as through one man sin entered the world, and death through sin, and thus death spread to all men, because all sinned"* (Romans 5:12).

When Adam and Eve sinned, the inherent propensity to sin entered the human race. Humanity became sinners by nature, because of the disobedience passed on from their parents (see v. 18; Hebrews 7:7-10). That nature is present from the moment of conception – making it impossible for humans to live in a manner that pleases God (see Psalm 51:5). Therefore, humans are not sinners because they sin – but rather they sin because they are sinners.

In God's plan of salvation it is very clear, that He intends the very meaning of the word, salvation to include our practical deliverance from sin, as well as forgiveness for our sins committed. In his book, *"The Normal Christian Life,"* Watchman Nee illustrates God's method in carrying that out. We inherited sin in our human nature from our parents. So, in God's plan of regeneration, He looks upon the old sin nature as a factory and sins as the product produced by the factory.[4]

He justifies us

- In the event of redemption, Christ's virgin birth, death and resurrection (blew-up the factory) so it no longer produces sins. He took our [believers] sins and gave us His righteousness (see 2 Corinthians 5:21). He saved us! Ponder this: "If God has destroyed the factory [your old sin nature] how can it possibly continue to produce sins?"

He sanctifies us

- In His process of sanctification, after the "new birth," (John 3:3), the believer has partaken of God's divine nature (1 Peter

44

1:4). We are now a new creation in the Lord's new [spiritual creation], united with Christ through faith in Him and commitment to Him (see 2 Corinthians 5:17; Romans 6:11; Ephesians 1:1; Philippians 2:1) in the new birth as the darkness of sin is dispelled by the light of the gospel [*the light of the knowledge of the glory of God*].

We are to grow in grace and the knowledge of our Lord and Savior, Jesus Christ (see 2 Peter 3:18). Folks this is our antidote for false teachers who boast in their error.

He supplies us

- Peter adds to that, *"Grace and peace be multiplied to you in the knowledge of God and of Jesus our Lord, as His divine power has given to us all things that pertain to life and godliness, through the knowledge of Him who called us by glory and virtue, by which have been given to us exceeding great and precious promises, that through these you may be partakers of the divine nature, having escaped the corruption that is in the world through lust"* (1 Peter 1:1-4).

He keeps us

- After all the attention necessarily given in the letter to the ungodly and their works of darkness, Jude concludes his letter by focusing attention on God and the theme of salvation which Jude desired to develop at the beginning (v. 3) and bolstered the courage of the children of God to know that Christ is fully able and would keep and protect them from *falling into the present apostasy* – who put their trust in Him (see Jude 24).

The Benediction

- We will close with a further word (vv. 24-25) from Jude. As a little boy I was taught that you should not leave the worship service until the benediction [the blessing] has been spoken over you. Jude's benediction/doxology stands as one of the most beautiful in the New Testament, notice:

Now to Him who is able to keep you
from falling,
And to present you faultless
Before the presence of His glory,
To God our Savior,
Who alone is wise,
Be glory and majesty,
Dominion and power,
Both now and forever
Amen.

Confirm by thoroughly studying the following New Testament benedictions:

- Romans 11:33-36
- Romans 16:25-27
- 2 Corinthians 13:14
- Hebrews 13:20, 21

CHAPTER SUMMARY: CHAPTER 4

1. God gave Adam _____ over His creation and he _____ the animals.

2. Adam and Eve had access to the tree _____ _____ in the garden.

3. Who was Lucifer _____?

4. The union of God and man is a new _____ having the life of God.

5. What is Genesis 3:15 called? _____.

6. If Satan could destroy the first eleven chapters of Genesis, what would be the results?

7. Jesus was raised under the _____.

8. _____ is our High Priest forever.

9. There is One that will keep you from _____.

10. Why did Jesus have to die as a man? Explain below:

CHAPTER 5

TWO FOUNDATIONS

"Therefore, as through one man's offense judgment came to all men, resulting in condemnation, even so through one Man's righteous act the free gift came to all men resulting in justification of life " (Romans 5:18).

Once sin was introduced into the life of Adam and Eve, the bliss of the Garden of Eden was gone. In the Garden they knew only goodness; they were comfortable in their physical bodies, in their sexuality, in their work, and in their relationship with God. However with the introduction of sin all of that changed. First, they were naked and ashamed a result of their now sinful nature (see Genesis 2:25).

I believe Adam and Eve passed on to their off springs, Cain and Abel, the story of God's love and mercy toward them though they deserved immediate death; He killed animals "made tunics of skin and clothed them" (see Genesis 3:21). Some theologians have expressed the thought that this was the beginning of the blood sacrifice as a way to God. The thought introduces a dichotomy of thought as reflected in Cain and Abel's worship (see Genesis 4).

Come let us worship

The Scripture speaks of the impact of sin even in worship. In fact their error in worship is still practiced today. "In the process of time it came to pass that Cain brought an offering of the fruit of the ground [which was cursed by God]." Abel also brought an offering, probably the same as Cain's (see Genesis 4:4-5).

However, concerning Abel's offering the writer of the Book of Hebrews said, "By faith," Abel offered to God a greater sacrifice than Cain, through which he obtained witness that he was righteous, God testifying of his gifts; and through it he being dead still speaks" (Hebrews 11:4).

While it is widely accepted that Abel also brought a lamb, we can't stop there in the explanation of why God accepted his sacrifice and rejected Cain's. The Word of God said it was "by faith." I believe Cain had as much knowledge of the offering as Abel, even in how he was to bring it, "by faith." However, he did it his way and like Cain so many today are trying to come to God in worship their way.

By Abel's action of bringing a sacrificial lamb according to his faith, God counted him righteous. The righteous bloodline was in Abel and not Cain. Cain rose up and killed his brother. God continued the righteous bloodline by raising up Seth. Through blood "By faith" is still God's way. However, it's through the sinless blood of Jesus Christ. Many individual Christians and churches are plagued *today* with the way of Cain prominently exercised so sincerely in their midst [sincerely wrong]! In Abel's faith we see him acknowledging that, *"without shedding of blood, there is no remission of sin" (see Hebrews 9:22).* Emphasis added.

God' plan of salvation

Repentance toward God and faith in the precious blood of Jesus Christ is God's only established way of humanity's reconciliation with Him. Christ's life for our life, that's what God demanded. After Christ finished His work of dying on the cross and rising from the dead; redemption for humanity was accomplished and available! The Father then looked not on our sin, but on His Son's blood.

God, the Son, Jesus Christ, the sinless Lamb fit the role perfectly; and from Genesis to Revelation His sinless blood runs through God's entire plan of redemption and reconciliation. He did it all by Himself!

In 1 Corinthians 6:20 and 7:23, we are told very clearly that, *"we are not our own and we were bought with a price.* That price being as Peter explains, *"You were not redeemed with corruptible things as silver and gold ... but with the precious blood of Jesus Christ"* (1 Peter 1:18-19). I reiterate apart from who Christ is and what He has done for us there is absolutely no other way that an individual can be reconciled to Father God! Jesus said of

Himself, *"I am the way, the truth, and the life. No one comes to the Father except through Me"* (John 14:6). The songwriter wrote, "There is a fountain filled with blood drawn from Emmanuel's vein. And sinners plunge beneath that flood lose all their guilty stain." Praise God! Thank you Lord!

I did it my way [Cain]

In his bloodless offering from the cursed ground without faith, Cain was saying by his action, I don't need a redeemer which is the same declaration heard in every corner of the American culture and wider society today. Cain knew the truth but refused to do what was right by it. The Scripture teaches, "To him who knows to do good and does not do it, to him [or her] it is sin" (see James 4:17). Paul admonishes, "Because what may be known of God is manifest in them, for God has shown it to them, so they are without excuse" (see Romans 19-21). Emphasis added throughout.

When Cain rejected the blood of the Lamb, the tree of the knowledge of good and evil and its true fruit came into full view for all to see. Counterfeit truth or empty headed tares had arrived. As stated earlier Cain was so angry of his rejection that he rose up [though God gave him a chance to repent] and killed his brother. Jesus said of Satan, *"He was a murderer from the beginning"* (John 8:44).

How was Satan able to influence Cain to join his troops? The answer in the Scripture also answers many questions concerning those in our midst who determines to do it their way. The Scripture explains,

> "Little children, let no one deceive you. He who
> practices righteousness is righteous, just as He is
> righteous. He who sins is of the devil, for the devil
> has sinned from the beginning. For this purpose the
> Son of God was manifested that He might destroy
> the works of the devil. Whoever has been born of God
> does not sin, for His seed remains in him; and he
> cannot sin because he has been born again of God.
> In this the children of God and the children of the devil are
> manifest: Whosoever does not love his brother, for
> this is the message that you heard from the
> beginning that we should love one another, not as
> Cain, who was of the wicked one and murdered his
> brother. And why did he murder him? Because his
> works were evil and his brother's righteous"
> (1 John 3:7-12).

The children of God are those who are born again and exhibit the truth by producing righteousness. In contrast the children of the devil who are not born again do not produce righteousness – simply because they cannot.

The children of God

The incarnation of God into the human race to do for us what we could not do for ourselves has been God's established plan from the foundation of the world. The Scripture says, God was in Christ reconciling the world unto Himself. The angel told the disciples to; *"Go stand in the temple and speak to the people all the Word of life"* (Acts 5:20).

I believe religion has been so superposed with laws and stereotypes by the world that true Christianity can no longer be identified as a religion. In fact it seems that the word Christian has suffered the same. The Scripture says "they were called Christians first at Antioch – Christian meaning "little Christ" or "Christlikeness" or "like Christ."

Today many people wearing the label Christian would not dare think of themselves as identifying with one of the three positions described above. Some would even be offended. More and more

Christians consider this to be politically incorrect especially in the public square, even though it is biblically correct.

The "life" makes Christianity more than mere religion; it is a life to be lived, eternal life. Therefore it is unique from all world religions, as they consist of obeying rules and laws with no interaction with their founder who are long dead anyway. Our Lord and Savior, Jesus Christ is also our living Founder; therefore He seeks a personal loving relationship with each of His children whom He has made righteous and gave eternal life. Jesus said, "You must be born again" (John 3:3).

God's purpose [to conform His children]

God's will is that His children be conformed to the image of Christ, His dear Son (see Romans 8:29). Now in the life of Christ, we have the love of God in our hearts and the Holy Spirit given to us forever. While we are a Spirit-filled supernatural people; we need other Spirit-filled children of God around us to administer grace sometimes to help us in the process of correcting our unhealthy thinking released through our attitudes and actions.

The theology of the early church reflected the God who acts, but today's theology reflects the God who spoke. Not only that, many have turned to the Bible itself rather than the Christ of the Bible. The central message remains the Person and work of Jesus Christ.

The Apostle Peter admonishes, "Grace and peace be multiplied to you in the knowledge of God and of Jesus our Lord, as His divine power has given to us all things that pertain to life and godliness, through the knowledge of Him who called us to glory and virtue, by which have been given to us exceedingly great and precious promises, that through these you may be partakers of the divine nature, having escaped the corruption that is in the world through lust" (2 Peter 1:1-4).

The genuine child of God is eternally secure in his or her salvation and will persevere and grow because they have received everything necessary to sustain eternal life through Christ's power. This "knowledge" is a strengthening form which implies a larger more through and intimate knowledge. The child of God's precious faith is built on knowing the truth about God. Jesus said, "I am the truth ..." As blood-washed children of God, we can be the vessels through whom Christ can address that problem in others.

In his book "*Sacrilege*" Hugh Halter suggests the doing away with discipleship for biblical apprenticeship. He advocates three things that provides checks and balance in biblical apprenticeship:

1. becoming just like Jesus,
2. doing what Jesus did, and
3. doing the above with the types of people Jesus liked spending time with.

He concludes, "When the people respond to you as they did Jesus. When they are drawn to you, seek you out for help, like you, respect you and want to live like you."[5]

I agree with the writer, discipleship like the words Christian, Christianity and born again have all been superposed until the many redefinitions can be very confusing.

In this book I want to come alongside the word Christian with "children of God" because we have a definite and clear biblical definition found in the Word of God.

They are children of God because:

- They are born again (John 3:3).

- They are being conformed to the image of Christ (Romans 12:2).

- They are righteous (2 Corinthians 5:21).

- They are led by the Spirit (Romans 8:14).

- They are reconciled with God and Christ (2 Corinthians 5:18).

Christianity is more than a religion it's a life in loving relationship with God and Christ by the Holy Spirit; while religions are all of works. Christianity is a life of walking in a personal relationship with the living Christ. The world's stereotypes of the Christian are not biblical, yet many Christians seem to love living within the bounds of their atheistic/ and humanistic definitions.

STUDY SUMMARY: CHAPTER 5

1. Adam and Eve were naked and _____ as a result of their sinful _____.

2. God accepted Abel's offering by _____.

3. Without _____ of _____ there is no remission.

4. Cain's offering came from the _____ which was cursed by God.

5. Jesus fits the role of a _____ _____ perfectly.

6. The children of God are born again and produces _____.

7. It is God's _____ that we be conformed to the _____ of His Son.

8. Jesus said of Satan, "He was _____ from the beginning.

9. Give three of the five reasons we are called the children of God:

   1. _____ 2. _____ 3. _____

10. Briefly explain "regeneration" in the space below:

SECTION TWO

SO GREAT SALVATION

CHAPTER 6

THE POWER OF GOD
UNTO SALVATION

*"For I am not ashamed of the gospel of Christ, **for
it is the power of God to salvation** for everyone
who believes, for the Jew first and also for the Greek"*
(Romans 1:16).

Paul tells us that the Gospel is "the power of God unto
salvation" – not the power of God "unto religion" or "good
living" or "good works" or "prosperity" but "unto salvation." Salvation
signifies saving – and for one to be saved, he or she must be lost! The
great need today is to get people to understand that they are lost!
Emphasis added.

"Lost" and "salvation" are two unpopular and unheard subjects in
many progressive-leaning sermons. More popular today is: "decision,"
and "unite with us," and "join the church and become a part of us."
"Let us make a better you." Few invitations these days are extended for
miserable, hell-deserving sinners to come forward in humble repentance
to receive Jesus Christ as Savior, and thus be saved from sin.

Salvation and the power of the Gospel signify:

- Redemption
- Justification
- Propitiation
- Forgiveness
- Sanctification
- Glorification

Salvation is in three tenses:

1. In the first tense, every born again believer *has been saved* from the guilt, and the penalty of sin (study Luke 7:50; 1 Corinthians 1:18; II Corinthians 2:15; Ephesians 2:5, 8; and II Timothy 1:9).

2. In the second tense, every born again believer is daily being saved from the dominion of sin (study Romans 6:14; 8:2; II Corinthians 3:18; Galatians 2:19, 20; Philippians 1:19; 2:12, 13; II Thessalonians 2:13).

3. In the third tense, every born again believer in the future will be saved entirely from the very presence of sin (study Romans 13:11; I Thessalonians 4:13-18; Hebrews 10:14; I Peter 1:5; and I John 3:2).

Implied in salvation are:

- Righteousness
- Deliverance
- Assurance
- Preservation
- Maturity
- Healing

Salvation is by grace through faith

Salvation comes by God's grace through saving faith alone. It is God's free gift. The Scripture says,

> *"For by grace you have been saved through faith, and that not of works, lest anyone should boast. For we are His workmanship, created in Christ Jesus for good works, which God prepared beforehand that we should walk in them" (Ephesians 2:8-10).*

The *grace* of God is the source of salvation; *faith* is the channel, not the cause of salvation. God alone saves. Salvation never originates in the efforts of people – it always begins in the *loving kindness of God.*

"Truly salvation is of the LORD" (John 2:9).

Acceptance of Christ

> *"But as many as received Him to them He gave the right to become children of God, to those who believe in His name: who were born, not of blood, nor of the will of the flesh, nor of the will of man, but of God" (John 1:12-13).*

The person who believes in His name meaning, Jesus Christ, which is what His name stands for – Jesus Christ our Lord, is salvation. In Exodus 3:14-15, God spoke to Moses and declared that He is the Eternal One. Only the Creator of all things can call Himself the, I AM. In the context of the above Scripture, it means to believe that Jesus is the Word, the Life, and the Light – that is, He is the Christ, the Son of God (see John 20:31).

As the, I AM, Jesus gave them the right to the legitimate entitlement to the position of children of God[6]. Look at God's love, by believing – under deserving sinners can become full members of God's family!

This new spiritual birth is not of physical blood parents, nor is the new birth of the will or flesh; that is, not of the individual's efforts, neither is the birth the will of man that is not by another individual. Each person must individually trust Christ for eternal life. Salvation is a gift to be received not a reward achieved through human effort.

The Fruit of the Spirit

Our spiritual growth as the children of God is to move from Christlessness to Christlikeness. Planted by the Spirit in our new nature are the fruit of the Spirit, Christ character traits which when fully developed in us makes us like Christ. The principle we now live under works on the basis of the finished work of Christ that provided a just basis for the Holy Spirit to permanently dwell within us and produce the life of righteousness.

He is free to live in our mortal bodies even though the sin nature [flesh] with its lusts is still in us. Yet, we no longer practice sin! The Christian still has the ability to sin, but he or she now has a healthy appetite for godliness. The dynamic is still there, but not the desire to sin. We can now say "no" to its lusts, temptations, and habits through Him who keeps us from falling.

To do this we must by faith remain fully dependent upon the Holy Spirit and not our own human strength and abilities. The Holy Spirit produces the righteous life in the child of God that is above the law's standard and pleasing to God. He forms the "fruit of the Spirit," which is one fruit comprised of these virtues recorded in Galatians 5:22-23:

Love – The Greek term is "agape" meaning the love of God, respect, devotion, and affection that leads to willing self-sacrificial service, and seeking nothing in return (also see 1 Corinthians 13; John 15:13; Romans 5:8; John 3:16-17).

Joy – is happiness based on unchanging divine promises and kingdom realities. It is the sense of well-being experienced by one who is in right relationship with God. In spite of unrelated circumstances (also see John 16:20-22).

Peace – is the inner calm that results from confidence in one's saving relationship with Christ. Like joy peace is not related to one's circumstances of life (also see John 14:27; Romans 8:28; Philippians 4:6-7, 8).

Longsuffering – refers to the ability to long endure the fragilities, offenses, injuries, and provocations inflicted by others and situations (also see Ephesians 4:2; Colossians 3:12; 1 Timothy 1:15-16).

Kindness – is tender concern for others reflected in a desire to treat others gently; just as the Lord treats all true children of God (also see Matthew 11:28-29; 19:13-14; 2 Timothy 2:24).

Goodness – is moral and spiritual excellence manifested in active kindness (also see Romans 5:7; 6:10; 2 Thessalonians 1:11).

Faithfulness – is the living, divine principle of inward and whole-hearted confidence, assurance, trust, and reliance in God and all that He says (also see Hebrews 10:19-38; 11:1, 6; Romans 4:17; 8:24; Revelation 2:10).

Gentleness – also translated "meekness" is a humble and gentle attitude that is patiently submissive and balanced in tempers and passions and in every offense; while having no desire for revenge or retribution (also see Psalm 25:9).

Self-control – is the restraining in the indulgence of passions and appetites (also see Proverbs 23:1-3; 25:16; 1 Corinthians 9:25-27; Philippians 4:5; 1 Thessalonians 5:6-8; Titus 2:2-3; 11-12; 2 Peter 1:5-6).

It's important that I repeat, love is the most important fruit formed by the Spirit. This is God's love [agape] and cannot be produced by any human efforts. Without love the other eight character traits are impossible. God's kind of love also allows the child of God to live a life above what is required of the law. The other eight are temporal – love is eternal!

First things first

> "Love the Lord your God with all your heart
> And with all your soul
> And with all your mind.'
> This is the first and greatest commandment.
> And the second is like it:
> Love your neighbor as yourself.'
> All the Law and the Prophets
> Hang on these commandments.
> (Matthew 22:37-40).

> Seek first the kingdom of God
> And His righteousness
> And these things shall be
> Added unto you
> (Matthew 6:33).

The fruit of the Spirit must be developed in us here while in this body – to go with your glorified body!

STUDY SUMMARY: CHAPTER 6

1. The _____ is the power of God unto _____.

2. The three tenses of salvation are:

   1.

   2.

   3.

3. _____   _____   and
   _____ are implied in salvation.

4. Salvation is a gift to be received; not a gift to _____.

5. The _____ of God is the source of salvation.

6. As the I AM, Jesus gave us the right to become _____ of _____.

7. The new spiritual birth is not of _____ parents nor of the will of the _____.

8. Each person must _____ trust Jesus Christ for eternal life.

9. The great need today is to get people to understand that they are _____.

10. Christ took my sins and gave me His _____.

CHAPTER 7

IT ALL BEGINS WITH LOVE

Jesus said to him, "You shall love the Lord your God with all your heart, with all your soul, and with all your mind. This is the first and great commandment. And the second is like it: "You shall love your neighbor as yourself" (Matthew 22:37-39).

When most Christians think of love, they usually think automatically in terms of developing love relationships toward their brothers and sisters in Christ. This is necessary in that God commands it of His children, and yet, this is not all that is involved in love.

There is another more important aspect of love. Each child of God must through the Spirit diligently cultivate and develop an individual relationship with our heavenly Father. Many Christians don't seem to realize that the Great Commandment is to love the brethren, but in the proper order only after first loving God. A lack of a proper biblical worldview and inadequate knowledge of the truth has some Christians:

- Expressing more love for the church building or others in the body of Christ than they express to God.

- Not comfortable expressing their love directly to the Father.

- Feel it's not politically correct to publically express love to the Father who loves them so much that He gave His only begotten Son to die on the cross in their place (see John 3:16).

- Substituting the various erroneous religious reports of individuals and groups and God, instead searching out the truth of God's Word for them self.

Unfortunately, however, this confusion is caused in large part by spiritual and biblical ignorance. This is the case with many in the family of God. If Jesus walked into your church in the flesh for the purpose of joining your Bible discussion; would we still be relaxed as we usually are just conversing about Him? One Sunday morning while my family and I attended worship

Service in the [Chapel at the U.S. Army Garrison in Yongson], Seoul, South Korea, suddenly while Chaplain Vaughn was preaching, all of the lights in the sanctuary dimmed, and a spotlight came on but fell short of fully revealing a man's full figure standing in the shadow. Gradually he slowly came into view. The man was dressed like most paintings we see supposedly of Jesus. He had the beard, long hair, robe and manner.

Gasps went up all over the sanctuary; and then quietness, all eyes were fastened on him While we were all trying to process the scene the Chaplain assured us that the man was a professional actor. What an effect! You might think, "Oh, I would have acted like Peter, Lord bid me to come to you!" God never fails to amaze me.

Develop an intimate relationship

God desires that His children know Him to the extent that they are in their closet most intimate relationship on earth with Him. Only then will His children come to know the Father in the Spirit as well as they know the people closes to them in the flesh.

**"A loving relationship with God flows
from a transformed heart!"
– Jay R. Leach**

Today many people express their love to the Father indirectly
by doing good works; but in these New Testament times
it is about *relationships*. In that day when those trying to
make it through their works stand before Christ, they will
be rejected by Him. Jesus said in Matthew 7:22, 23):

*Many will say to Me in that day,
Lord, Lord,
have we not prophesied in your name,
cast out demons in your name,
and done many wonderful things in your name?
And then I will declare to them,
I never **knew** you;
depart from Me,
you who practice lawlessness!*

The Greek word used here for knew is *ginosko (ghin-oce'-ko)* which
means "to know by experience or effort; knowledge as the result of
prolonged practice; knowledge grounded in personal experience. Jesus
is saying:

*"I never got to know you, for you did not cultivate the
fruit of love and develop an intimate, loving relationship
with Me." "You stand in no relation to Me."*

That's the correct report from Christ Himself? Therefore, it
behooves each person who claims to be a true child of God if not
doing so already – begin immediately to develop a love relationship
with the Father by cultivating this eternally-important fruit of love

today. In the next chapter, we will more fully discuss our increasing love for God, through abiding in His Son, Jesus Christ.

Develop experiential knowledge of God rather than just information about Him.

The consummation of love

Genuine love for one another [children of God] proves our spiritual birth and our relationship with God. Concerning many other biblical truths, church people testify sheepishly, "I love everybody!" "Well what about God, "I've got to work on that one:"

- If we would just get it right. It is impossible to know God intimately without loving others, for God is love (see John 4:8).

- Therefore, anyone in whom God dwells reflects His character. To claim to know God while failing to love others is a false claim.

- Other examples that contain contrasts between *words* and *works* or saying one thing and doing another (study thoroughly 1 John 1:6-10).

- The love of God for His children was visibly demonstrated through Jesus' finished work on the Cross on our behalf.

A check of history

In all of history no one has demonstrated a love for people as did Jesus. In Him we see a radical inclusivity and acceptance of rich and poor people, old and young people, educated and uneducated people, sick and healthy people.

Notice His love expressed at the Cross for His mother, the soldiers who crucified Him, and the thief on the cross. It is the unconditional, self-sacrificing, all-inclusive, irrational love that melts the hardest heart and draws that person to the Father:

- What would happen if we were radically inclusive with the people we meet during the course of our daily work and activities?

- If we really believed as children of God in the schools, neighborhoods, and workplaces, that our primary job is to love people, no matter who they are, their ethnicity, economic status, lost or found, rich or poor, old or young?

Jesus says, "All men will know that you are My disciples, if you love one another" (see John 13:35).

There are three components to salvation, a person can fake conversion, go down a dry devil and come up a wet devil – but of the three components, love cannot be faked. As children of God, the perfected [mature] expression of our love – produces confidence as we anticipate the coming judgment of the world. Anyone without the unconditional [agape] self-sacrificing love of God – is not a blood-washed child of God!

Out of His mercy

Notice, the past tense of the verb *saved* in this passage indicates that the child of God's salvation has already happened in the past, [at the cross] the gift of God. Remember, we cannot do anything to earn salvation. Only God can grant new life and save us from the predicament the whole human race inherited from Adam's sin:

- Out of His grace *[unmerited favor – giving us what we do not deserve]* through faith, we have been saved and not of anything we have done

- Out of His mercy *[not giving us what we do deserve]* God gave His Son for us while we were yet His enemies. He *loved us* long before *we loved Him.*

In this love, God has sent
His only begotten Son
into the world that we might
live through Him.

In this is love,
not that we loved God,
but that He loved us
and sent His Son
to be the propitiation
for our sins.

Beloved,
if God so loved us,
we also ought to
love one another.

— 1 John 4:9, 11

Love for one another referring to our fellow children of God proves our spiritual relationship with God. Paul admonishes,

"For we ourselves were also once foolish, disobedient, deceived, serving various lusts and pleasures, living in malice and envy, hateful and hating one another. But when the kindness and the love of God our Savior toward man appeared, not by works of righteousness which we have done, but according to His mercy He saves us, through the washing of regeneration and renewing of the Holy Spirit, whom He poured out on us abundantly through Jesus Christ our Savior ...." (Titus 3:3-6).

One another ministry

There are some fifty or more what I call "one another ministries" recorded in the NIV. Thoroughly study each Scriptural application:

* "Be at peace with each other" (Mark 9:50).

69

- "Wash one another's feet" (John 13:14).
- "Love one another" (John 18:34).
- "Love one another" (John 13:35).
- "Love each other" (John 15:12).
- "Love each other" (John 15:17).
- "Be devoted to one another in brotherly love" (Romans 12:10).
- "Honor one another above yourselves" (Romans 12:10).
- "Live in harmony with one another" (Romans 12:16).
- "Love one another" (Romans 13:8).
- "Stop passing judgment on one another" (Romans 14:13).
- "Accept one another, then, just as Christ accepted you" (Romans 15:7).
- "Instruct one another" (Romans 15:14).
- "Greet one another with a holy kiss" (Romans 16:16).
- "When you come together to eat, wait for one another" (1 Corinthians 11:33).
- "Have equal concern for one another" (1 Corinthians 12:25).
- "Greet one another with a holy kiss" (1 Corinthians 16:20).
- "Greet one another with a holy kiss" (2 Corinthians 13:12).
- "Serve one another in love" (Galatians 5:18).
- "If you keep on biting and devouring one another ….. you will be destroyed by each other" (Galatians 5:15).
- "Let us not become conceited, provoking and envying one another" (Galatians 5:26).
- "Carry one another's burden" (Galatians 6:2).
- "Be patient with one another in love" (Ephesians 4:2).
- "Be kind and compassionate to one another" (Ephesians 4:32).
- "Forgiving one another" (Ephesians 4:32).
- "Speak to one another with palms, hymns, and spiritual songs" (Ephesians 5:19).
- "Submit to one another out of reverence for Christ" (Ephesians 5:21).
- "In humility consider others better than yourselves" (Philippians 2:3).
- "Do not lie to one another" (Colossians 3:9).
- "Bear with one another" (Colossians 3:13).
- "Forgive whatever grievances you may have against one another" (Colossians 3:13).

- "Teach one another" (Colossians 3:16).
- "Admonish one mother" (Colossians 3:16).
- "Make your love increase and overflow for one another" (1 Thessalonians 3:12).
- "Love one another" (1 Thessalonians 4:9).
- "Encourage one another" (1 Thessalonians 4:14).
- "Encourage one another" (1 Thessalonians 5:11).
- "Build one another up" (1 Thessalonians 5:11).
- "Encourage one another daily" (Hebrews 3:13).
- "Spur one another on toward love and good deeds" (Hebrews 10:24).
- "Encourage one another" (Hebrews 10:25).
- "Do not slander one another" (James 4:11).
- "Don't grumble against one another" (James 5:9).
- "Confess your sins to one another" (James 5:16).
- "Pray for one another" (James 5:16).
- "Love one another deeply from the heart" (1 Peter 1:22).
- "Live in harmony with one another" (1 Peter 3:8).
- "Love one another deeply from the heart" (1 Peter 1:22).
- "Live in harmony with one another" (1 Peter 3:8).
- "Love one another deeply" (1 Peter 4:8).
- "Offer hospitality to one another without grumbling" (1 Peter 4:9).
- "Each one should use whatever gift he has received to serve one another" (1 Peter 4:10).
- "Clothe yourselves with humility toward one another" (1 Peter 5:5).
- "Greet one another with a kiss of love" (1 Peter 5:14).
- "Love one another" (1 John 3:11).
- "Love one another" (1 John 3:23).
- "Love one another" (1 John 4:7).
- "Love one another" (1 John 4:11).
- "Love one another" (1 John 4:12).
- "Love one another" (2 John 5

By sheer numbers it is very apparent these "one another" Scriptures are important to God. Certainly with the uncertainty, fear and frustration in our communities today this type of ministry is imperative. Love for one another was in view as Jesus exhorted His disciples,

> *"A new commandment I give to you, that **you love one another; even as I have loved you,** that you also love one another. By this all men will know that you are My disciples, if you have love for one another" (John 13:34, 35).* Emphasis added.

In many church circles very little or no emphasis is placed on teaching and modeling this kind of love (unconditional love). The Greek term for this kind of love is *"agape."* Agape promotes ministry that is not seeking for its own or anything in return. When a church expresses this kind of love, faithful sharing and burden bearing takes place as the work of the church [inside] and the church's work [outside] glorifies God.

James 2:14-26 warns, "faith without works is dead." If a person testifies that he or she has faith, but does not the works of righteousness, that person's testimony is vain, the same is true for the church. Salvation is not of works – but salvation works! Genuine faith will naturally produce good works, activated by love.

God sent His Son

> *"For God so loved the world that He gave His only begotten Son, that whoever believes in Him should not perish but have everlasting life. For God did not send His Son into the world to condemn the world, but that the world through Him might be saved" (John 3:16-17).*

What has love got to do with it? Love has everything to do with it! God is so merciful! When I was in Vietnam I believed that America was special in God's sight; in spite of the bad press I still think we are God's best – for the sake of right! I was stationed in Nancy, France, a few clicks from Paris in the early 60's when I first heard of and experienced "the ugly American." The Marshall Plan had rebuilt Europe from the destruction of World War II, and they were on their way. Thank you America – now leave! The largest Communist party outside of Russia at that time was in France.

Though there were incidents with soldiers clashing periodically within the populace, the Christian consensus of America was present there, even influencing our politics. God and prayer to God was in the top five recommendations for problem solving as instructed in our leadership and counseling manuals.

Character guidance classes were a part of our heritage. The influence of world leaders raised up by God was prevalent throughout the world. Between January 1959 and January 1965 I spent five years in Europe [two years in Germany and three in France] split by my being assigned to Fort Bliss Texas for nine months in 1962. Perhaps you wonder why all the reminiscing, well having done extensive travel throughout Europe two things was highly noticeable even then:

- Atheism

- The very high influx of Muslims especially in France.

We see the same storm cloud over Europe moving on our nation's *horizon*. Although Jesus died for the whole world! Listen to the Scripture,

> *"Blessed is the nation whose God is the Lord,*
> *The people He has chosen as His own*
> *Inheritance"*
> – Psalm 33:12

God's love is not restricted to any one nation, or to any spiritual elite individual or group. At His first coming, Jesus came so that the world through Him might be saved. When Jesus comes again, He will come in judgment upon those who refused His offer of *salvation*.

Our greatest need

The Scripture speaks of three inseparable friends [faith, hope, and love], the greatest of which is love. God is love and love reflects the greatness of God.

> *God's love is shed broad in our hearts by the Holy*
> *Spirit who is given to us* (see Romans 5:5).

Love is the greatest need of our life experience. Therefore it is no doubt the greatest gift we can give. Even if He is correcting or discipling us, He is still loving us. The Scripture says, "Whom the Lord loves He chastens" (see Hebrews 12:6-8). Period historians recorded the beauty of the early church, "O how those Christians love one another!"

That distinction of the early church was very appealing. It drew people to know the Lord, who was the source of love. It is this deposit of God's love in us that draws others to the life in Christ that God intended. There is a great need for the local churches to take inventory and adjust their priorities in these last days to the attractiveness God intended. God is love. "We love Him because He first loved us" (see 1 John 4:19).

Many spiritual, emotional, and mental problems could be resolved, if caring Christians would accept their biblical responsibility to show authentic love [agape]. In these perilous and seemingly hopeless times for many in and out of church; it is easy to find opportunities to proclaim the acceptable year of the Lord. In fact it is almost impossible to avoid it.

The media seems to be poised everywhere to exploit the fear, uneasiness, and uncertainty of the people. However this climate presents an open door for the children of God to quiet the hearts of the fearful with a reassuring Word of hope.

CHAPTER SUMMARY: CHAPTER 7

1. Each child of God must cultivate and develop an individual _____ with our heavenly Father.

2. Today many Christians lack a proper _____ _____ and have inadequate knowledge of biblical _____.

3. Salvation is _____ _____ works.

4. Develop experiential knowledge of God rather than just _____ about Him.

5. _____ for one another _____ our relationship with God.

6. Love [agape] promotes ministry that is not _____ for its _____.

7. Jesus came the first time so that the world _____ _____ might be saved.

8. Hebrews 12:6-8 says, "Whom the Lord loves _____.

9. God is _____.

10. The beauty of the early church was their _____ for one another.

SECTION THREE

BEAR

MUCH

FRUIT

SECTION THREE

BRIAN

MUCH

CHAPTER 8

ABIDE IN ME

"I am the true vine, and My Father is the vinedresser. Every branch in Me that does not bear fruit He takes away; and every branch that bears fruit He prunes, that it may bear more fruit" (John 15:1-2).

"If you abide in Me, and My words abide in you, you will ask what you desire, and it shall be done for you. By this My Father is glorified, that you bear much fruit, so you will be My disciples" (vv. 7, 8).

Two things were said of His Spirit-filled disciples; that fulfilled these verses in the early Church. And they are just as true for His Spirit-filled children who love Him today:

1. "They turned the world upside down."
2. "The Lord added to the Church."

I'm sure that this was due to God's being glorified by the disciples' lives in Christ Jesus through the Spirit of truth.

Jesus said, "He who believes in Me, the works that I do he will do also; and greater works than these he will do, because I go to My Father. Jesus laid down definite principles which the disciples followed and His promised results came to pass. Notice, Jesus said,

- Love Me
- Keep My commandments
- Believe in Me
- Ask in My name

And I will pray the Father and He *will* give you another Helper, that He may abide with you forever – the Spirit of truth in essence, you will do greater works because:

- The Father will give you another Helper – the Spirit of truth
- You know Him.
- He dwells with you and will be in you.
- I will not leave you orphans,
- I will come to you.
- You will see Me.
- He who has seen Me has seen the Father.

Further, He said, "Because I live, you will live also. At that day you will know that I *am* in My Father and **you in Me and I in you.** He who has My commandments and keeps them, it is he who loves Me. And he who loves Me will be loved by My Father, and I will love Him and manifest Myself to him" (study carefully John 14:12-21).

The Spirit of truth

Jesus had accomplished the greatest works possible, including raising the dead. How could He say that the children of God would do greater works? This question causes much discussion in Sunday schools and Bible studies today. Why? Because a great percentage of the church tries to understand the spiritual truths including what Jesus said here, by natural means [what they see, taste, smell, hear, or feel]. As a result Satan puts up a smoke screen to keep many in darkness.

In verses vv. 16-17, Jesus speaking of the Spirit of truth – **whom the world <u>cannot receive</u>** *because it neither sees Him nor knows Him; but you know Him .... He dwells with you and will be in you."*

So looking spiritually at what Jesus said is seen in the extensive work the apostles did. Jesus' work on earth was confined to Palestine. The apostles preached everywhere and saw thousands converted. Peter's message on the Day of Pentecost brought more people to Jesus than did Jesus' entire earthly ministry. The disciples were able to do this work because Christ ascended to the Father **and sent the Holy Spirit to <u>empower</u> them.** All three members of the Godhead, Elohim, were represented in this mighty event: Jesus prayed to the Father who would send the Holy Spirit. In the Great Commission Jesus promised His disciples,

> *"But you shall receive power when the Holy Spirit has come upon you; and you shall be witnesses of Me in Jerusalem, and in all Judea and Samaria, and to the end of the earth" (Acts 1:8).*

The Children of God's mission

This was power for a new task – to take the gospel to the ends of the earth. Christ's command to His disciples to *tell others* about Him no matter what! God empowered His disciples to *be faithful witnesses* even when they faced the most violent opposition. Jesus also promised that He would not leave nor forsake **us,** but would be with **us always even to the end of the age** (see Matthew 28:20; John 14:18). Jesus fulfilled that promise in the Person of the Holy Spirit, who dwells **within** the true children of God:

> *"But these things I have told you, that when the time comes, you may remember that I told you of them. "And these things I did not say to you at the beginning, because I was with you. "But now I go away to Him who sent Me and none of you ask Me, "Where are you going?" But because I have said these things to you, sorrow has filled your heart. Nevertheless I tell you the truth. It is to your advantage that I go away; for if I do not go away, the*

> *Helper will not come to you: but if I depart, I will send Him to you" (John 16:4-7).*

The Conflict begins

I was pastor of a middle-sized church while I was in graduate school. Some of my most senior members of the church could not understand why I needed more education – their explanation was the Holy Spirit would teach me. Thus we have the unnecessary conflict between the Holy Spirit and education. I will simply conclude this argument with the fact that the Apostle Paul had both and I'm sure you will agree God was able to do great things through him (study Acts and the Pauline letters).

The first parents, Adam and Eve tried to hide their sin with fig leaves (study carefully Genesis 1-3); then with the invention of the printing press came the Holy Bible with the Garden of Eden story of Adam and Eve. Soon the literature book came along with Paradise Lost. The distinction between the two is the heavenly inspiration of the Holy Spirit in the writing of the Bible; while literature is earthly and therefore temporal. Thus we end up with two explanations concerning all things. They are:

- The biblical/ heavenly [Spiritual guidance]

- The secular/ earthly [natural guidance]

Therefore we have the truth of God's Word versus humanities' secular word and temporal explanation. It is so sad that so much error concerning the Holy Spirit has arisen in the body of Christ. Some believe He is some type of energy, influence or force. Many Christians are deceived by these earthly explanations, and therefore never experience a personal relationship with the Holy Spirit.

At the same time confusion has caused many to fear the Holy Spirit and never come to the reality – **that a viable true Christian life is impossible without a relationship with the Holy Spirit. The same is true for the life of any church.** The Holy Spirit does influence the life of the Christian, and He is revealed as the power of God, but His influence is a personal one – that will "keep you from falling" (see Jude 24).

STUDY SUMMARY: CHAPTER 8

1. Briefly explain in the space below the two things that were said of Jesus' disciples in the early church:

   a.

   b.

2. I will pray the Father and He will give _____.

3. The Spirit of Truth will dwell _____ you and _____ you.

4. According to Acts 1:8, what did Jesus promise His disciples?

5. The world cannot receive the _____ of _____.

6. The apostles were tasked to take the gospel to _____ _____ of the earth.

7. Peter's sermon on the Day of Pentecost won _____ souls.

8. Research shows that only 25% of Christians believe the _____ _____ exists.

9. Adam and Eve tried to hide their nakedness with fig _____.

10. There is one that will keep you from _____ (Jude 24).

CHAPTER 9

THE PROMISE REVEALED

"For by one Spirit we were all baptized into one body, whether Jews or Greeks, whether slaves or free: and have all been made to drink into one Spirit" (1 Corinthians 12:13).

Jesus explained to His disciples the benefits of the coming of the Spirit:

- With the coming of the Spirit, believers have the Holy Spirit dwelling within (vv. 7-15).

- With the coming of the Spirit believers can have full joy (vv. 16-24).

- With the coming of the Spirit believers can have fuller knowledge (vv. 25-28).

- With the coming of the Spirit believers have the privilege of peace (vv. 29-33).

- With the coming of the Spirit believers experience the unity of the body of Christ through the Baptism of the Holy Spirit.

His purpose in coming

It's important to note – the coming Holy Spirit **would not** be given to the world, but to believers. However, when He comes:

- He will convict *[convince]* unbelievers of **sin** (vv. 8-9) through the believers who witness about Christ (15:26, 27). Our witness should not focus on **sins** (adultery, pride, and other sins, per se) – but on the full payment that Christ has made for all sin. We should focus on receiving the full pardon; which is the only cure for the disease of sin.

- He will convict *[convince]* unbelievers of **righteousness** (v. 10) and the need of righteousness. Jesus' work on the cross was completely righteous. This was demonstrated by the empty tomb which signified the Father's satisfaction with the righteous payment and His acceptance of Christ in His presence.

- He will convict *[convince]* unbelievers of **judgment** (v. 11). Satan, the ruler of this world, rules in the hearts of **unregenerate people** and blinds their minds. Even though Paul had many strengths of his own, he wanted to be counted among those who relied on God's strength to impart wisdom that is of God and not humanity (study carefully 1 Corinthians 2:6-8).

Satan was judged at the Cross, and the Holy Spirit would convince people of the judgment to come. Satan has been judged, so all who side with him will be judged with him. There is absolutely no wiggle room or neutrality. A person is either a child of God or a child of the devil.

The Holy Spirit is real

The church was born on the Day of Pentecost, when the Spirit of God baptized all of the believers into the body of Christ (Acts 2:2). The Scriptures tell us that the moment we commit our lives to Jesus, the Holy Spirit comes into our lives and seals us as children of God. From that time forward the Spirit is working out His purposes in our lives. He is,

- Helping us in times of temptation.
- Giving us strength when we are weak.
- Providing wisdom when we are making decisions.
- Convicting us when we sin.
- Transforming us into the image of Jesus Christ.

We are to daily surrender our lives to Him; which allows Him to work in and through us:

- To point out where you missed the mark.
- To take time to confess the sin to God.
- To ask for forgiveness.
- To ask for strength to turn from it.
- To strengthens you in your personal holy habits of Bible study, prayer, meditation, and application.

The Holy Spirit and the Word of God work in tandem to perfect us.

A Spiritless version

In a conversation with a young man who had converted from Islam to Christianity, I was shocked at his attitude toward the Holy Spirit. He accepted the Father and the Son, but did not believe the Holy Spirit is a real Person in the Godhead. So the idea that God is at work *in us* by the person of the Holy Spirit was foreign to him.

A few days back as I was scanning some past issues of Charisma magazine my eyes fell upon an article in the August 2014 issue titled, "You're not an Extra" by Jeff Kennedy. I had taken the young man as an exception to the rule concerning the Holy Spirit, however according to this article he has become is really the rule today.

In the article Kennedy reported a finding by The Barna Group that only 25% of Christians in America believe in the *existence* of the Holy Spirit! What does that say about the other 75%? Many churches are dull and earthy and without spirit. In that same report Barna also found that younger generations are less likely to embrace the Spirit. As I stated in an earlier section there is a mass exodus from the church of those ages 18 to 34 years old in America. It seems that many church leaders have forgotten that it is the Spirit who draws and quickens people to Christ and salvation?

In his letter 2 Timothy 3:1-9, Paul prophesied to Timothy, the church and to us that in the future certain conditions would mark the last days of the age. The picture he presents concerns undeniable characteristics of the end times. Reading through the chapter is similar to viewing our daily evening newscast. You compare, as Paul chimes out:

Perilous times will come (v, 1):

Though times have been perilous in all ages, I'm sure we all agree that recent times are harder, more grievous, fearful, and the intensity of ungodliness increases daily on a worldwide scale. Certainly the reason the last days will be perilous was because the world will be godless! Notice how the last days Paul speaks of sounds like a picture of today.

A Godless World

For the sake of time, many churches program out the work of the Holy Spirit in their worship and other services. People want to be in control, so they set a time limit on the services, however to do that they must exclude the Holy Spirit because He is uncontrollable. No wonder so many are leaving the church and Christianity is declining. We have come to a place where we don't want God in the services.

Many would rather rely on secular science and technology than the divine revelation of God as is given by the Holy Spirit. Many churches' concepts and programs are wrapped so tight that there is no place for the Holy Spirit's agenda. Have we forgotten the command not to grieve the Holy Spirit? How can we effectively build Christ's church without His own appointed Superintendent; whom He sent to lead and guide us in getting the job done?

Research reveals that a great number of churches in America are stumbling along at the edge of darkness due to spiritual and biblical ignorance. Likewise a look across their membership rolls exposes too many people who are living in the same sin as those outside the church; having fallen into the snare of Romans 1: 20-21.

> *"For since the creation of the world His invisible attributes are clearly seen, being understood by the things that are made, even His eternal power and Godhead,* **so that they are without excuse, because, although they knew God, they did not glorify Him as God, nor were they thankful, but became futile in their thoughts, and their foolish hearts were darkened."**
> Emphasis added throughout.

This Scripture is telling us, what God provided in Creation is too great and too marvelous to be denied. Yet, with all of His manifested power in the world in Creation, people **refuse to recognize their Creator; and worship, or glorify Him as God.** Emphasis added.

He gave them up

For a period of time I fell into gross sin. I walked into a sinful situation with my eyes wide open. Under heavy conviction from the very beginning, I faced a decision; I knew in my heart that if I choose wrong, God would have given me up [period]. I was terrified at the very thought of that happening!

Like the prodigal son who incidentally was still a son even while he was in the pig pen acting like a pig. His father received him back as his son. I to arose and came back to My Father and my wife with much repentance and remorse for my sinful and selfish act. Praise God both God and my family met me with great love, forgiveness and expectation! God's grace and mercy brought me through. Though forgiven I sorrow over the circumstances created by my inattentiveness while in sin for a season. I love God and my wife more than ever; and through their *love* and *mercy* – I am at this place in time.

Through the years, I have counseled many Christians who came to the same crossroad I did. [I know the reason God sent them to me]. My counsel to any believer is: when we knowingly or unknowingly get involved with any sinful situation don't be strong and stand, be weak and run and like Joseph leave your coat if necessary [read his story in Genesis 39:1-23].

Run and don't look back! Believe it or not you are *physically* and *spiritually ruining not only for your life, but also the lives of your spouse, other present loved ones, and planting generational curses and strongholds upon your family for generations to come!* Emphasis added throughout.

While I could have described my sinful state with other terms, *"selfish"* points to "me" "I," because it was I who hung around the edge and Satan snared. Be careful! We love to preach about the son in the pig pen, but believe me there are some pigs in the father's house, note the other brother! The snare or trap or door to sin is immediately activated once we begin to rationalize *sin*, by saying things like:

- I deserve this opportunity or affair or you fill in the blank _____ (?).
- I can handle this.
- No one will be hurt by it.
- No one will ever know.
- It'll be my only sin.
- The big lie is, "I'm somehow still in God's will and grace."
- You might consider it a small thing because the state or national law has made it legal, so everybody is doing it.

Don't count on where you perceive others to be in relation to God and His judgment. God is sovereign and unless you repent, this might be your very last chance before, "God gives you up!" Today, lots of Christians are falling into known sin, but it seems:

- They have absolutely dulled their consciences [yet, know right from wrong].

- They are making decisions and not considering the fallout and circumstances that will alter their lives forever!

- The churches are excluding the Holy Spirit and His ministry; and hiring life coaches, and employing various philosophical and psychological "How to tactics" to replace the Word and Spirit of God.

I pray for those in the Household of Faith today who knowingly turn off the Holy Spirit's conviction [for us it's His *convincing* us to repent and turn back to obeying God's moral law]. That's mercy! I pray for pastors, who have continued in their positions, yet feel no leading toward addressing these violations of God's moral laws and allowing moral relativism to reign in the church just as it does in the culture:

- Some do so out of the fear of men.

- Some don't want to rock the bank book.

- Some actually feel it's none of their business.

- Some know it's compromising the truth of God's Word, but fear the wrath of the people more than God.

- Some have been convinced by opposing forces atheists, humanists, and those found in Romans 1:1-21 that we've already lost the war. Don't give up. If you will notice some pastors are addressing these moral issues with biblical truth! Their church is growing and their altars are full. People want truth and that no doubt goes double for the millennials. Our God is alive and much LARGER!

I won't mention that I am not being politically correct, because the media, academia, and the culture have already deemed it incorrect for anyone to speak on these issues unless they are in agreement. In fact, it's sad to say, many of the brethren agree with them. As God's Spirit-filled pastors and teachers, we know that we are *biblically correct* to do so – we know the truth, let's just obey, and use our "free speech"!

I have mentioned this in other sections and it bears repeating. A Barna pulpit research poll among a large number of pastors revealed that only 5% of pastors across America address issues such as abortion, adultery, same-sex marriages, cohabitation, multi-divorces and multi-remarriages, family dysfunctions and much more. Why aren't the churches defending God's truth on these issues? Are you one of His spokespersons or not? The 95% who admitted that they never mention these issues to their congregations are really promoting the humanists' agenda! They are definitely counting on the Christians to be quiet! Sad to say many pastors agree that it's none of their business.

Most professionals consider themselves eternal students who stay knowledgeable and relevant on cultural issues pertaining to their people – perhaps most clergy think they have enough. Many believe and act according to what the anti-Christian culture and media tell them no matter whether it's right or wrong. This anti-Christian hostility is rooted in calling, *"evil good and good evil"* (see Isaiah 5:20).

Unsurprisingly according to research the ratio of pastors with and those without a biblical worldview is about the same. Matter of fact everyone has a worldview, and it is based on what you believe about life, issues of the day, how you handle them, where you are going upon death and everything else. The source of these views has a direct bearing on our conduct, behavior and outlook on life

For instance most people in America today have secular worldviews because of the various mindsets from family, friends, peers the media, education, government and many other sources available to form them. Some people joke about how wonderful the television is as a baby-sitter. Of course they will cry later. There's an old saying, the hand that rocks the cradle rules the world "view."

Taking action

Certainly we often urge our people to pray and stand up on the issues – we should also encourage them to take action:

- America is based on freedom of speech and religion, so we can't allow anyone or any group to remove us from the discussion.

- Each church should teach a biblical worldview – a [truthful] one for all.

- As God's people of love – we should show some love!

- Support Christian businesses, public and professional individuals who stand up for the truth of God's Word. Chick-fil-A, Hobby Lobby and Faith Driven Consumer's founder Chris Stone a brand strategist who helps companies reach consumers whose faith is serious enough to direct their purchasing habits.

- Every church should have church approved spokes-brethren who study the person and platforms and worldviews of local and national candidates vying for the public's vote. Additionally they should prayerfully examine the biblical validity of the current issues of the day – keep the congregation informed. This should not be done during worship services.

- We should take a stand in a way that would please God.

Over the years the biblical worldview and Christian consensus upon which have helped keep this nation safe and strong has eroded to very dangerous level s. Those pastors and teachers who choose not to address the moral issues also fail to teach a biblical worldview; which in actuality denies biblical truth, promotes the secular agenda and drives many in the group called millennials [ages 11-34] away from the church. The millennials want and need reality and truth. So, when addressing these issues please leave off the sour jokes, exaggerations and clichés such as, "I know what you are going through!" "Do you really know?"

CHAPTER SUMMARY: CHAPTER 9

1. With the coming of the Holy Spirit believers experience the _____ of the body of Christ.

2. The coming of the Holy Spirit _____ _____ to be given to unbelievers, but to believers.

3. He will convict the unbelievers of _____, _____, and _____.

4. We are to surrender our lives _____ _____.

5. People refuse to recognize their _____ or worship, or _____ Him as God.

6. Churches are excluding the _____ _____ and His ministry.

7. The anti-Christian hostility is rooted in calling "_____ good and _____ evil."

8. Each church should teach a _____ worldview.

9. The group called millennials ages _____ to _____ are leaving the church.

10. America was founded on _____ of speech.

CHAPTER 10

NOT FOR PASTORS AND PARENTS ONLY

"A little leaven leavens the whole lump. I have confidence in you, in the Lord, that you will have no other mind; but he who troubles you shall bear his judgment, whoever he is" (Galatians 5:9, 10).

Whether we admit it or ignore, God is our only hope for fixing the situations we face in our Country and churches today. Making the situation so very terrible are statistics reflecting that only 25% of Christians in America believe in the existence of the Holy Spirit! Undoubtedly that same statistics reflect 75% who have never heard of Him, do not believe He exists or simply reject Him. Even though the Word of God distinctly makes it clear; that the Holy Spirit is the Helper that Christ promised would come; and be in those who are His children on earth to carry out the work Jesus began in them and at the same time build His church through them (see John 16:7, 13).

A little leaven

Leaven symbolizes the *intruders,* with their false philosophies, doctrines and satanic influences toward damaging the children and the things of the true and living God. Today, just as it was in Paul's day the attack centers on dispelling the truth of God's Word for selfish purposes and Satan's gain.

Secular humanism is an organized philosophical system relatively new, but its foundations can be found in the ideas of classical Greek philosophers such as the Stoics and Epicureans. Those philosophical views looked to humanity rather than the gods to solve human problems. It is important that every child of God know the subtle ways that secular humanism is manifesting itself in every facet of society as it very subtly undermines Christianity and the biblical worldview. Their secular generals have declared war on God, Jesus Christ, the children of God and the things of God everywhere.

They have won many battles over the past forty or fifty years. The secularists are now imbedded in the highest offices and positions with great influence on the citizenry across the United States through the spread of their atheistic views in colleges, universities, judicial districts, public school systems, governmental agencies at all levels, and sadly they are often joined by some false faith leaders who are encouraging "millennials" to trade in their biblical convictions for a progressive gospel filled with compromise.

While America sleeps these secular generals are engaging in and promoting a war between Christianity and Secular Humanism. What kind of jump does that give atheists and humanists on Christians and Christianity? There are three Humanists Manifesto dated 1933 (I) signed by John Dewey; 1973 (II) and 2003 (III).[8]

Well, while the church was sleeping their materialistic/ hedonistic agenda birthed in academia through such notable educators as John Dewey who referred to *humanism* as a *Common Faith,* advocated an ecumenical belief system based on humanistic values compatible with his views of ethics and biology.[9]

And his contemporary Charles Francis Potter who authored, *Humanism: A New Religion,* which stated the movement's objective to replace a theistic religion with an atheistic one.

His thesis, considered education to be Humanism's most powerful ally, **every American public school is a school of Humanism.** He surmised theistic Sunday schools, meeting one hour a week, and teaching only a fraction of the children has no chance against a five-day a week school program of humanistic teaching.[10] What does all of this equate to? These are the kind of people of whom Paul spoke in Ephesians 2:11-13 who found themselves in the position of "having no hope, and without God in the world."

Secular objectives

1. Secularists reject the existence of God and the supernatural.

2. Secularists believe evolution is the only way to explain the existence of life.

3. Secularist's values have been imbedded into every facet of American society to the extent that we have become unconscious of them!

4. Secularists no longer claim to be a religion; yet humanism has become the very essence of religious culture.

5. Secularists see moral values as relative; changing and varying from person to person.

6. Secularists view man as the supreme being of the universe.

7. The adherents of humanism take their fundamental beliefs to be self-evident.[11]

> The Scripture warns, *"See to it that no one takes you captive through philosophy and empty deception, according to the traditions of men, according to the elementary principles of the world, rather than according to Christ"* (Colossians 2:8 AMP).

Are secularists atheists?

Secularists are generally non-theists. They typically describe themselves as nonreligious. They hail from widely divergent philosophical and religious backgrounds. The demonic punch line of humanism is: *"what-ever-it-is seems the only way to be."*

As stated earlier, secular humanists do not rely upon gods or other supernatural forces to solve their problems or provide guidance for their conduct. They rely instead on the application of reason, lessons of history, and personal experience to form an ethical/moral foundation and to create meaning in life.

Secular Humanism places trust in intelligence rather than divine guidance.

I stated earlier, that in recent years humanists have become so well-placed in our society occupying powerful positions which affect all levels of marriage and family life, education, government, media, and the market place:

- They no longer feel the need to conceal themselves or their beliefs; because their influence in many areas has a greater impact on the culture than the influence of the church.

They no doubt are convinced that it is too late for Christianity and the pro-moral people in this country to do anything about it. Though they have entrenched themselves; it's not too late to root them out!

God's counter: Salt and Light

> Jesus said, *"You are the salt of the earth, but if the salt loses its flavor, how shall it be seasoned? It is then good for nothing but to be thrown out and trampled underfoot by men. You are the light of the world. A city that is set on a hill cannot be hidden. Nor do they light a lamp and put it under a basket, but on a lampstand, and it gives light to all who are in the house. Let your light so shine*

> *before men, that they may see your good works and glorify*
> *your Father in heaven"* (Matthew 5:13-17).

Salt is both a preservative and a flavor enhancer. I'm sure Jesus was mainly referring to its use as a preservative in this passage. Pure salt cannot lose its flavor or effectiveness, but the salt that is common salt can if contaminated with other minerals. A godly life gives convincing testimony of the saving power of God; that brings glory to Him (see 1 Peter 2:12).

God's people are to uphold that which is right and oppose that which is wrong. When we do that, we set the example for all around us to see. We must oppose humanism because its teachings are contrary to the teachings of God's Word. We must come to understand, and help others to understand, that human wisdom such as that of humanism is folly. Listen to the Scripture:

> *For it is written, I will destroy the wisdom of the*
> *wise, and discernment of the discerning will I bring to*
> *naught, where is the wise? Where is the scribe? Where is*
> *the disputer of the world? Have not God made foolish the*
> *wisdom of the world? For seeing that in the wisdom of God*
> *the world through its wisdom knew not God. It was God's*
> *good pleasure through the foolishness of the preaching to*
> *save them that believe* (1 Corinthians 1:19-21).

God wisely established that men could not come to know Him by human wisdom. That would exalt man; so God designed to save helpless sinners through the preaching of a message that was so simple the "worldly wise" deemed it nonsense. In Romans 1:19-20, the Scripture makes clear that man is conscious of God's existence, power, and divine nature through general revelation; because God has sovereignly planted the evidence. However:

- They would not acknowledge God. God holds all humans responsible for their refusal to acknowledge Him (see Acts 8:26-39; 10:1-48; 17:17).

- They chose not to glorify God which is his chief end; but failing to do so is the greatest affront to the Creator. They are without excuse (see Leviticus 10:3; 1 Chronicle 16:24-28; Romans 15:5, 6).

- "Though they knew God, they neither glorified Him as God nor gave thanks to Him" (see Romans 1:21). The Apostle Paul taught that man's rebellion against God began with failure to express thanks. Lack of gratitude characterizes the unbeliever who fails to acknowledge God and His standards of righteousness, as Paul goes on to say in Romans 1. Children of God should stand in sharp contrast, constantly expressing their thankfulness to God for who He is and what He has done. As we do this our thanksgiving will be replaced by praise. Have you noticed how readily we are to praise others and express our approval? "Great meal!" "You look great!" God wants our praise!

- Their search for meaning and purpose was futile; only producing vain, conclusions. Their hearts were darkened. When any person rejects the truth, the darkness of spiritual falsehood replaces the truth (see John 3:19, 20).

The power of two or three

I am convinced that we can intercede in prayer with much assurance that we will be heard by our God:

> *"Ask, and it will be given you; seek, and you will find; knock and it will be opened to you: For everyone who asks receives, and he who seeks; finds, and to him who knocks it will be opened"* (Matthew 7:7, 8).

> *"Pray without ceasing"* (1 Thessalonians 5:17).

Pray without ceasing does not mean that we go around all day in a constant flurry of prayer. True prayer is an attitude of the heart:

- We should feed the hidden person of the heart with spiritual food; in the same manner that we seek to feed the body (see Matthew 4:4; 1 Peter 3:4).

- We should make sure that our spiritual garments are in order, just as we are careful over the physical garments that clothe our physical body (see Colossians 3:7-15).

- We drink physical water, but we should drink the spiritual water of life as well that Christ offers (see John 4:13-14; 7:13).

Spiritual guidance through intense study for "truth" in God's Word, exposes the teachings and stated objectives of secular humanism to enough people, we can turn back to a moral consciousness in this great nation. Christ is our only hope!

"The wicked shall be turned into hell and all nations that forget God" (Psalm 9:7).

CHAPTER SUMMARY: CHAPTER 10

1. The Holy Spirit is the Helper that Christ _____ would come.

2. Humanism's views look to humanity rather than the _____ to solve human problems.

3. The _____ are embedded in high places all across America.

4. The Secularists are promoting a war between _____ and _____.

5. _____ _____ hailed as the father of modern education was a proponent of secular humanism.

6. The humanistic objectives remain to replace Christianity with _____.

7. Every public school in America is a school of _____.

8. Secularists reject the existence of _____ and the supernatural.

9. Secularists view _____ as the supreme being of the universe.

10. Secular Humanism believes that values are _____.

SECTION FOUR

THE CHILDREN
REVEALED

CHAPTER 11

THEY WILL SHINE

"For I am determined not to know anything among you except Jesus Christ and Him crucified. I was with you in weakness, in fear, and in much trembling. And my speech and my preaching were not with persuasive words of human wisdom, but in demonstration of the Spirit and of power, that your faith should not be in the wisdom of men but in the power of God" (1 Corinthians 2:2-5).

In the last chapter, we saw the results of what happens to any church that excludes the Holy Spirit and His ministry. The void will be filled with:

- Your overreliance on strategy, planning, and programming led by the most knowledgeable thinkers and commentaries available.

- Your worship is professionally programmed and produced to create a certain experience; which is not a problem in itself.

- Your problems lie in leaving God out of your planning; and at the same time trusting in your own weak abilities.

- Your solutions are limited to logic and debate to resolve problems

Rather than preparing for a decision by listening in prayer for the guidance and power of the Holy Spirit; the prevailing mode of operation in most churches today rely heavily on current rationally determined information, programmed flowcharts, and packaged productions. These methods of operation leave no place for the spontaneous instructions and interruptions of the Holy Spirit.

Transformation

Our most skillful sermon preparation, props, and technics without the power of the Holy Spirit surging through us are useless to others. God transforms our humble knowledge into an incarnation of truth. The truth of the cross is the gospel, the Good News about Christ's death and resurrection for our sins. The gospel penetrates to the core of our self-centeredness. For those who exalt self, the message sounds absurd. But for those who bow humbly in the faith, it becomes the power that is able to snatch them from death and impart eternal life (see Romans 1:16-18). Captivated by the Truth:

- We must invite others to receive the gospel and become true children of God.

- God's plan of salvation does not conform to the world's priorities. In fact to them it seems foolish. Yet in reality, eternal life is more valuable than all the fame, wealth, and success pursued by the world.

- Serving Christ our Lord, loving and growing in Him allows His strength to be manifested in our weakness.

- Many are preaching such fleshy messages today, "How to grow and become a better you" "Five steps to find who you are through self-evaluation." However, the point of the true message of the cross is that all human efforts to find favor with God fall shamefully short (see Romans 3:9-18).

Transformed from the inside out

It is God's desire that we give 100% of ourselves [spirit, soul, and body] to Him. He demands it! I heard a preacher some years ago say, "God does not deal with apartments; He wants the whole building or none." He was illustrating how God wants our whole being; and He will not settle for anything less.

A beautiful picture of transformation is seen in the transforming process a worm into a beautiful monarch butterfly. The worm is spun within a cocoon, then through a process known as "metamorphosis" [*meaning to change to something else*] the worm is changed into something else namely [a butterfly]. A lesson can be gained from the process through a story. The story is told of a young man walking through a park. He observed a butterfly struggling to break free of its cocoon, it seemed to be struggling for its life.

As he reached to help it, a shout came from behind from a lady walking on the trail behind him, "Don't touch it!" It was too late, he broken the butterfly free; it fell to the ground. He asked the lady, "What happened?" The lady explained to him that the struggle is a major part of the metamorphosis process. The butterfly's newly developed wings are exercised and strengthened through the struggle.

The process of becoming

Like the butterfly in the illustration, our strength for the journey comes as the Holy Spirit carries us through the process of life's experiences and struggles out of which our love and trust in the Lord matures. We will not properly develop without the struggles. The process of transformation [our becoming a new creation *in Christ*] is of the Lord.

Many Christians and churches are paralyzed with fear and inactivity. Fear negates faith; and without faith it is impossible to please God. This is one of the major strategies Satan deploys. In the first place he tries to stop every person from becoming a mature child of God. However, once one becomes; the devil tries to keep them in the inactive reserve ranks.

He has deceived many Christians into thinking that being saved means they can just sit back and enjoy the Lord and do absolutely nothing while they wait for His return. This attitude is growing in this country as more and more churches exclude the Holy Spirit and the supernatural from their Christian experience, thus forfeiting their relationship and godly assigned work.

Today, Satan through his people takes full advantage of those fearing peers and public opinion. Other earthly deceptions such as "political correctness" "your Christianity is a private matter" "moral relativism" "inclusively" "the new tolerance" "evolution" imbedded throughout our national society, promotes the humanistic agenda swaying the majority of the populace to believe: **"what-ever-it-seems-is-the-ONLY-way-to-be!"**

God's people are to uphold that which is right and oppose that which is wrong. We set the example for all in our area of influence to see. We must oppose humanism because its teachings are contrary to the teachings of God's Word.

More and more people are deceived as the culture continues to kick God, Christ, and the life of godliness to the curb for secular humanism. What is so sad here is the fact that most people drawn into this philosophy are not aware that it has happened. Many have never heard the word "humanism!" It's no wonder the Lord said, "The harvest is plentiful, but the workers are few. Ask the Lord of the harvest, therefore, to send workers into his harvest" (see Luke 10:2).

Everyone in the kingdom of God is called to work. This work is not to be saved but because we are saved. Paul told the Christians in Ephesus that doing good works for Jesus is the very reason God saved them: "For we are God's workmanship, *created in Christ Jesus to do good works,* which God prepared in advance for us to do" (Ephesians 2:10). Emphasis added.

God not only saved you to do good works, but He has given each of His children a specific task for which He called and gifted you to do. Our role is to be led and enabled by the Holy Spirit to do what He directs us to do. God not only gives us power to do the work (see Acts 1:8); but the desire for godly wisdom to do it. Paul told the Philippians,

"Continue to work out your salvation with fear and trembling, for it is God who works in you to will and to act according to His good purpose" (Philippians 2:12-13).

Who are the wise?

"Those who are wise shall shine
Like the brightness of the
firmament,
And those who turn many to
righteousness
Like the stars forever and ever"
------ Daniel 12:3

Who are the wise? Paul tells us that the wisdom of the world is foolishness with God, and the foolishness of God is wiser than the wisdom of the world. Further, he tells us, "..... If a man thinks himself to be something, when he is nothing, he deceives himself" (Galatians 6:3).

In 1 Corinthians 1:19-21, the Scripture declares, "I will destroy the wisdom of the wise, and discernment of the disconcerting will I bring to naught. Where is the wise? Where is the scribe? Where is the disputer of the world? Has not God made foolish the wisdom of the world? For seeing that in the wisdom of God the world through its wisdom knew not God, it was and is God's good pleasure through the foolishness of preaching to save them that believe."

Solomon declares, "The fear of the Lord is the beginning of knowledge ...." (Proverb 1:7). In James 1:5 we are told, "If any of you lack wisdom, let him [or her] ask of God .... and it shall be given to him [or her]." All true wisdom comes from God. In James 5:20 we read,

"Let him [or her] know that he who turns a sinner
from the error of their ways will save a soul from death
and cover a multitude of sins."

Research statistics show that some 2 billion people in the world who have never heard the saving gospel of Christ. Then there are increasing billions around the world trapped in false religions and philosophies; who unless countered by the power of the gospel of Christ will be led to eternal hell!

Human wisdom at war with God leads people away from Him; if it is not founded on biblical truth (study Romans 8:7). Knowing how high the stakes are should motivate every child of God to work aggressively in pursuing unregenerate people everywhere. Even one sin is enough to condemn a person to hell. James' use of the word *multitude* emphasizes the hopeless condition of lost unregenerate sinners.

The good news of the gospel is that God's forgiving grace, which is greater than any sin; is available to those who turn from their sins and exercise faith in the Lord Jesus Christ. We learn from Scripture:

1. That true wisdom, the gift of God, comes from the Holy Spirit by prayerfully studying and meditating on the Word of God.

2. That the fear of the Lord is the beginning of knowledge.

3. That he [or she] who wins souls is wise.

4. That the wise [soul winners] shall shine as the brightness of the stars forever.

In the 24th chapter of Matthew, Jesus pointed out that one of the signs of the end will be false prophets and false teachers, preaching error and wrongly dividing the Word.

If no one goes

I stated earlier, we hear a lot from ministers here in the United States concerning their successes at winning many souls for Christ. In spite of the few, most churches it seems have programed themselves out of this godly and purposeful mission. Another topic voiced here in this country is "Revival!" Revival doesn't happen by simply sitting around hoping it happens. Revival comes when the true children of God decide to fully give their past, present, and future to do whatever it takes to proclaim the good news everywhere!

In Romans 10:14-15, the Bible clearly lays out the obvious mission for each of us by asking,

> *"How, then, can they call on the one they have never believed in? And how can they believe in the one of whom they have never heard? And how can they hear without someone preaching to them? And how can they preach unless they are sent?"*

I've heard it stated this way 'some go, some pray, and some pay," but everyone is involved. This does not happen by us just standing by waiting on a sovereign move of the Spirit to come along and blissfully carry us on the journey. No, no it takes a lot of love, humility, sacrifice and hard work! Paul told the Corinthians,

> *"I worked harder than all of them, yet not I, but the grace of God that was with me"* (see Corinthians 15:10).

Later, he summarized some of the troubles he had to face in his ministry. Study carefully 2 Corinthians 11:23-28. Notice the number of times the word "danger" appears in this one passage. Paul gave his all in serving the Lord, and he knew what hard work was.

It seems an overemphasis has been put on grace and prosperity in the American churches, so the believers are lulled into thinking their job is to just lay back and wait on the unmerited favor to begin flowing [for many in dollars and cents].

I by no means belittle God's grace or prosperity, I cherish both of them, but experiencing both is meant to produce just the opposite effect in our lives, than what is perceived by most people. His grace should motivate and empower us to serve our Lord and Savior, and pray that He would prosper us with resources so we can make Him known everywhere!

Faith and Work

In an earlier chapter I stated that we don't work to be saved, but we work because we are saved. In a brief review of the parables of Jesus, you will notice that our works are very important to God. Therefore, it is important to note:

People only get to heaven by repenting, being "born again" and in so doing becoming children of God. It is only by the precious blood of Jesus that our sins are forgiven and we are reconciled to a righteous relationship with our Heavenly Father.

However, if you have truly been born again, the evidence that you have Jude 3 faith is demonstrated by whether or not you have borne fruit for the kingdom of God. The gospel is not only your means to get to heaven, but it also provides the greatest motivation for our works. If you really know the Lord, you can't just sit around and watch the world go to hell in a hand basket. James stated it very clear:

> *"What does it profit, my brethren, if someone says he has faith but does not have works? Can faith save him? If a brother or sister is naked and destitute of daily food, and one of you says to them, "Depart in peace, be warmed and filled," but you do not give them the things which are needed for the body, what does it profit? Thus also faith by itself, if it does not have works, is dead. But someone will say, "You have faith, and I have works." Show me your faith without your works, and I will show you my faith by my works. You believe that there is one God. You do well. Even the demons believe – and tremble! But do you want to know, O foolish man, that faith without works is dead? You see then that a man is justified by works, and not by faith only"* (James 2:14-20, 24).

James explanation here in no way contradicts Paul's very clear teaching that Abraham was justified before God by grace alone through faith alone (see Romans 3:20; 4:1-25, Galatians 3:6, 11). James on the other hand, is emphasizing how the saved child of God proves that salvation before others.

If people can see no changes in our lives; they have no right to believe that we are saved. His teaching perfectly complements Paul's writings; salvation is determined by faith without works, but saving faith leads to works (see Ephesians 2:8, 9)demonstrated by faithfulness to obey God's will alone (Ephesians 2:10).

Satan's deceptions have led many to believe that being a Christian is a matter of what we say with our lips; it involves what we do with our life! We may never equal the deeds of those people of God recorded in Hebrews 11, but by the things we say and do day by day. Faith that does not lead to works is *dead* faith and not *living* faith. Notice Jesus' example in 1 John 3:17,

> *"But whoever has this world's goods, and sees his brother in need, and shuts up his heart from him, how does the love of God abide in Him?"*

The only way true faith can be expressed in the Christian's life is by practical loving obedience to the Spirit and Word of God.

Again, faith that does not lead to works is not saving faith! It's so sad to say, there are multitudes of professing Christians and church members who have this *"dead faith."*

- They profess with their lips – but their lives deny what they profess. The apostle Paul explained this truth when he wrote to Titus,

- *"They profess that they know God, but in works they deny Him"* (Titus 1:16).

- True children of God are *"a peculiar people, zealous, of good works"* (Titus 2:14).

- This is why Paul exhorts, *"Examine yourselves as to whether you are in the faith; prove yourselves"* (2 Corinthians 13:5).

Certainly, the passages I expressed above in no way means that a true child of God never sins (carefully study 1 John 1:5-10): However, it does mean:

- That he or she does not make sin a practical habit in their lifestyle.

- That a true child of God focuses on bearing fruit for the glory of God.

- That he or she walks in a manner that pleases Him.

- That God deserves all of the praise, glory and honor!

CHAPTER SUMMARY: CHAPTER 11

1. Churches are relying heavily upon rationally determined _____.

2. The truth of the Cross is the Good News about _____ death and _____ for our _____.

3. We must invite people everywhere to _____, _____ the gospel and become _____ of God.

4. The gospel of Christ penetrates the core of our _____ _____.

5. God's plan of salvation seems _____ to the world.

6. More and more churches in America are excluding the _____ _____.

7. Everyone in the kingdom of God is called to _____.

8. Statistics show some 2 billon people in the world who never _____ the saving gospel of _____.

9. We don't work to be saved, but we _____ because we are _____.

10. Satan wants to push God, Christ and the children of God to the _____.

CHAPTER 12

BUILD YOURSELVES UP

"Building yourselves up on your most holy faith; praying in the Holy Spirit. Keep yourselves in the love of God, looking for the mercy of our Lord Jesus Christ unto eternal life" (Jude 20, 21).

Jude wrote in anticipation of the rise and increase of false teachers' and apostates' attacks on the name of Jesus Christ and His Church. He challenged the children of God everywhere; to build themselves up in the most holy faith:

- Each individual is to insulate themselves in the truth of God's Word. The Bible is the source of spiritual cleansing and growth. The church is the pillar of truth; therefore, church leadership must insure the teaching of these truths is carried out for the members at every level of membership. The apostle Paul exhorts,

   "So now, brethren, I commend you to God and to the Word of His grace, which is able to build you up and give

you an inheritance among all those who are sanctified" (Acts 20:32).

- He exhorts, *"Praying always with all perseverance and supplication for all saints"* (Ephesians 6:18).

    Here Paul introduces the general character of the child of God's prayer life. Continuously in prayer and supplication in the Spirit – focused on submission and the will of God. This is urgent for all saints not just the leaders, but all saints.

Jude called these apostates dirty spots, filth on the garment of the church. They promise spiritual life, but they are empty clouds; which bring the hope of rain, but actually deliver nothing but dryness and death (see Proverbs 25:14). An apostate is a defector from the truth:

- They have known the truth.

- They have given some show of affirmation to the truth.

- They oppose the truth and undermine it.

- They reject truth in the end.

- They undermine faith and corrupt truth such persons pose a dangerous threat to the health and welfare of the church.

- They strive to appear friendly, likable, and religious; that's why Jesus compares them to ravenous wolves in sheep's clothing (see Matthew 7:15).

- They may actually start out meaning well, but apostates never get past being double-minded. Their shallowness and worldliness makes it impossible for God's Word to take root (see Matthew 13:20-22).

- Despite whatever temporary appearance of spiritual life they might display, they are incapable of producing real fruit, and they eventually fall away.

- When false teaching goes unchallenged, it breeds more confusion and draws more shallow and insecure people into the church.

- Obviously, these people hurt the cause of Christ tremendously.

People who embrace apostasy are destroyed by it. Notice five out of seven churches in Revelation 2-3, were either beginning to defect from the faith or were already apostates. Sardis was already apostate and Laodicia was moving swiftly toward final rejection of truth. Christ's central message to all but two of the churches included a mandate to deal with apostates in their midst

The battle for truth

The battle for truth in the church has always been very difficult; but it is a very necessary conflict today. In the church:

- Most members don't care about the presence of false doctrine.

- Most members don't see it their duty to fight against apostasy.

- Most members want open inclusivity, tolerance, acceptance of opposing ideas and moral relativism is running rampart.

- Many members reject the few key gospel doctrines regarded as absolutely essential to true Christianity.

- A great number of church leaders today, are far more likely to express their displeasure and indignation at someone who calls for doctrinal clarity and accuracy than to firmly oppose some self-styled apostate who is attacking some vital truth of God's Word.

- For various reasons today many churches are bowing to the secular consensus, religious rituals, good works, and legalism over sound doctrinal truth and the ministry of the Holy Spirit.

Speaking the truth

Today those who are built up in the faith and love to speak the truth of God's Word are not popular. However, no matter what happens, we are to be obedient to God's will, God's word, and God's way:

- Speaking the truth in love.

- We cannot be discouraged by what we see around us in the culture and retreat to the security of the four walls nor let the culture remove us from the conversation.

- The world so desperately needs the light of God's children.

- Things that were unimaginable thirty or forty years ago have become the norm today. In many instances local churches have bowed to the pressures of the world, the flesh, and the devil.

- Insulated by the true faith and truth of God's Word; the children of God must put on the whole armor of God, stand up, stand fast, and take action as directed by the Spirit of God.

The line of demarcation

> *"In this the children of God and the children of the devil are manifest: Whoever does not practice righteousness is not of God, nor is he who does not love his brother"* (1 John 3:10).

A very distinct line of demarcation has been drawn between the children of God and the children of the devil as marked by *righteousness* and *love*. As God's children we have no authority to compromise or confuse God' Word. We are to rightly divide the

Word. The righteous children of God do not practice sin. The children of the devil are *unrighteous* and *without love*.

There are some people in the local churches who have faked conversion, and even faked baptism, but they can never fake love! Many are denying the power of the Holy Spirit and living defeated lives in His absence. This is coupled with the absence of the Word and prayer.

The children of the devil are trying to exclude the Holy Spirit from the church and reinstate legalism and religious forms of the flesh. "It doesn't take all of that" is their watchword. Their assignment is to secularize the church which would destroy it. When Satan gets a Christian or local church thinking and operating in the flesh – the battle is over. John similarly wrote,

> *"Do not love the world or anything in the world. If anyone loves the world, the love of the Father is not in him [or her]. For everything in the world – the cravings of sinful man [woman], the lust of the eyes and the boasting of what he or she has done – comes not from the Father but from the world. The world and its desires will pass away, but the man or [or woman] who does the will of God lives forever"* (study carefully 1 John 2:15-17). Emphasis is mine.

The absence of love for the world must habitually characterize the love life of the children of God who have genuinely been "born again." God not the world must hold the first place in our lives (carefully study Matthew 10:37-39; Philippians 3:20).

The Spirit of truth

Jesus told His followers,

> *"But when the Helper comes, whom I will send to you for the Father, the Spirit of truth who proceeds from the Father, He will testify of Me"* (John 16:7).

The Holy Spirit is working into us the image of Christ. We shall be like Him (carefully study Romans 8:29; Ephesians 1:4, 5, 11). One day we will all stand before the judgment seat of Christ and give an account for our lives.

Today is the time to repent, before it's too late! "In the past God overlooked such ignorance, but now He commands all people everywhere to repent. For He has set a day when He will judge the world with justice by the man He has appointed. He has given proof of this to all men by raising Him from the dead" (see Acts 17:30-31).

CHAPTER SUMMARY: CHAPTER 12

1. Jude challenged saints everywhere to build _____ up in the most holy _____.

2. Each individual is to _____ themselves in the truth of God's Word.

3. Members at all levels are to _____ themselves in the truth of god's Word.

4. An apostate is a _____ from the truth.

5. To embrace apostasy is to be _____ by it.

6. In the Book of Revelation, the churches of _____ and _____ were moving swiftly toward final rejection of truth.

7. Most church members don't care about the presence of _____ _____.

8. Most members don't see it their duty to _____ _____ apostasy.

9. The world so desperately needs to see the _____ of _____ _____.

10. The Holy Spirit is working into us the _____ of _____.

CHAPTER 13

THE CHILDREN MANIFESTED

"Whoever commits sin also commits lawlessness, and sin is lawlessness. And you know that He was manifested to the away our sins, and in Him there is no sin. Whoever abides in Him does not sin. Whoever sins has neither seen Him nor known Him. Little children, let no one deceive you. He who practices righteousness is righteous. He who sins is of the devil, for the devil has sinned from the beginning. For this purpose the Son of God was manifested, that He might destroy the works of the devil. Whoever has been born of God does not sin, for His seed remains in him; and he cannot sin because he has been born of God. In this the children of God and the children of the devil are manifest: Whosoever does not practice righteousness is not of God, nor is he who does not love his brother" (1 John 3:4-10).

The requirement of righteousness

These verses convey the true child of God's practice of righteousness. The verb "commits" in verse 4 lends the idea of making a habitual practice. Though sin is incompatible with the believer, we do have a sin disposition, and do commit sins and need to confess our sins. However this is not an unbroken pattern in our lives:

> "If we say that we have no sin, we deceive ourselves, and the truth is not in us" (v. 8).

> "If we confess our sins, He is faithful and just to forgive us our sins and to cleanse us from all unrighteousness" (v. 9).

> "My little children, these things I write to you, so that you may not sin. And if anyone sins, we have an Advocate with the Father, Jesus Christ the righteousness" (2:1).

There are reasons for a true child of God not habitually sinning:

- Because it goes against the moral law of God.

- Because he or she has a built-in guard [the new nature] against habitual sinning.

- Because it is incompatible with Christ's finished work. He died to sanctify [make holy] the child of God.

- Because it is contrary to Christ's work of breaking the dominion of sin in the believer's life.

Shall we continue in sin?

Paul exclaims, "Certainly not!" In the last section we dealt with righteousness or [justification] based on the free grace of God. So we are saved by grace through faith alone, and not of anything we've done ourselves. Christ took my sins [and yours] in fact the whole world's sins upon Himself on Calvary and gave us His righteousness (see 2 Corinthians 5:21; John 3:16). My conversion is a one-time event completed in the past. I am counted dead with Him and therefore risen with Him. We need to believe it, receive it and take action (study Romans 10:9-10).

Christ died to sin in two senses:

1. In regard to sin's penalty – Christ met its legal demands upon the sinner.

2. In regard to sin's power – Christ broke the power of sin forever over those who belong to Him. And His death will never need repeating (Hebrews 7:26, 27; 1 Peter 3:18).

Paul's point is that believers have died to sin in the same way. Therefore, he or she lives to God – for His glory!

- He or she reckons [count] yourselves to be dead indeed to sin, but alive to God in Christ Jesus our Lord (v. 11).
- He or she does not let sin reign in their mortal body, that you should obey it in its lusts (v. 12).
- He or she does not present their members as instruments of unrighteousness to sin (v. 13).
- He or she [presents] themselves to God as being alive from the dead (v. 13).
- He or she [presents] their members as instruments of righteousness (v. 13).
- Sin shall not have dominion over you – for you are not under law but under grace (v. 14).

Dead to sin – alive in Christ

As the children of God, we are to live a life of purity that far exceeds the standards of the world. Our lives are to be perfectly pure. Now, before you throw this book in the trash can hear me out. At the center of our experience is the life-giving *Helper* that Jesus promised to send from the Father, in the Person of the Holy Spirit and His ministry in and through us.

There are those among us who believe and teach that the Holy Spirit came on the Day of Pentecost and returned to heaven after the event. This group relies on science, reason, and technology through their five senses to find solutions to their problems and circumstances. In reality, this is the same approach the world uses. The Scripture says,

*"The **love of God** has been shed abroad in our hearts through the **Holy Spirit which** was **given** unto us **forever** (Romans 5:5).*

*"If any man [or woman] **does not have** the Spirit of Christ, he [or she] is none of His"* (Romans 8:9). Emphasis added throughout.

It is no wonder that the Pentecostals are growing faster than mainline churches around the world. My wife and I experienced working alongside Pentecostal missionaries in Panama/ Costa Rica and in South Korea. One major factor is the supernatural aspect:

"These signs shall follow them that believe

What this equates to is being involved in ministry that is impossible accept God does it through us. In America we have had access to medication for everything from the common cold to cancers, strokes etc. It comes natural for us to seek out these solutions. That's what we are familiar with; but that is not the same in the majority of the countries of the world. Hope gained through receiving the preaching of the gospel gives the people faith to believe for their salvation, healing or whatever their need may be. Especially when considering all of the privileges we enjoy in this country, but not readily available in many of those countries. In spite of all the efforts made otherwise, I believe America will soon experience a widespread need for healing ministry on the local church level.

At the same time we have experienced a Spiritual power surge for [souls and healings] throughout the Bread of Life Ministries' areas of influence. Only God can do these things. Rather planned or unplanned the rich are getting richer and the poor are getting poorer in this country. At the same time, both "compassion" which means "to

126

come alongside" and "charity" meaning "love" are being redefined the same way as other familiar words connected with biblical principles. Either they are secularized or redefined.

In addition to that the old habit of mechanically throwing money at the problem thinking somehow it will go away has actually created more social problems:

- Rampart illegitimacy
- Over-extended Government entitlement programs
- People below the radar – receiving financial aid, food stamps, and Tax returns without seeking employment.
- Deficient in national defense dollars

What is so sad is the fact that the majority of the people in the categories above live below the churches' radar also. Many of the people caught up in these situations are not interested in what we are doing in many local churches because whatever it is excludes them. They should be able to see God in what we are doing. The world should be able to see the difference that Christ makes in the lives of individuals, families, churches and areas of influence outside.

Christ does not expect His church to just live in peace with everybody, and spend all of their time creating busy work within the four walls. In fact, just the opposite is true – for the gospel is a powerful and abrasive message that confronts sin and the sinner head-on. Jesus said,

> "Do not think that I came to bring peace on earth. I did not come to bring peace but a sword. For I have come to set a man against his father, a daughter against her mother, and a daughter-in-law against her mother-in-law; and a man's enemies will be those of his own household" (Matthew 10:34-36).

Christ made it clear that though He is the "Prince of Peace," no child of God should think that this life is free of conflict. Therefore, if you or your church is not responding to God by attempting things that can only be accomplished through Him, then you are not exercising saving faith.

CHAPTER SUMMARY: CHAPTER 13

1. Jesus Said, the _____ has _____ from the beginning.

2. Rather one is a child of God or of the devil is determined by:

   a.

   b.

3. If we say that we have _____ _____ we deceive ourselves and the _____ is not in us.

4. A law of man is not automatically approved of God's _____.

5. There are those who believe the _____ _____ came on the Day of Pentecost then _____ to _____.

6. The love of _____ has been shed abroad in our hearts through the Holy Spirit which was _____ to us forever.

7. The world should be able to see the _____ Christ makes in the _____ of individuals _____ and _____.

8. Christ does not expect His Church to just _____ at peace with _____.

9. The gospel is a powerful and _____ message that confronts sin and the _____ head-on.

10. Every church should be attempting things that can only be accomplished _____ _____.

CHAPTER 14

A FRUITFUL FAITH

"According as His divine power
has given unto us
all things that pertain
unto life and godliness,
through the knowledge of Him
that has called us to
glory and virtue:"
– 2 Peter 1:3

The key word in 2 Peter is "knowledge," and the danger that burdens Peter and likewise the saints today is false teaching. Satan is a serpent desiring to deceive as many of God's children as he can, to do so he is no longer the lion in the street seeking whom he may devour through persecution; which actually has always cleansed and strengthened the church.

Notice, in Peter's day, Satan has changed his tactic and slithered into the church through false teachers. False teaching weakens the church and ruins its testimony. The only weapon to fight false teaching and the devil's accusations and lies is the truth of God's Word, which is why Peter is emphasizing spiritual knowledge.

Salvation is a personal experience, with Jesus Christ whom one comes to know through faith. So we must have a faith that knows, a faith that grows and a faith that shows:

A faith that knows (1:1-4)

It is not enough simply to know [Gk. *Ginosko*[12]] about Christ; we must know [Gk. *Epiginosko*[13]] Him in a personal relationship (Philippians 3:10). When we put our faith in Him, He gives us His righteousness (2 Corinthians 5:21). He becomes our Savior – it is a personal experience.

In this letter, Peter emphasizes the Word of God. God has given us His Word, this "precious faith" of God that we might live godly lives. In the Bible, we have all that we need for life and godliness. Please keep in mind, the writings of teachers and preachers can help us better understand the Bible, but only the Bible can impart life to our souls. The child of God has been born into God's family and has become *"partakers of divine nature* on the inside. People who try to live "like Christ" on the outside, but lack the divine nature on the inside, are deceived and defeated. Notice the Scriptural description of false Christians:

- They have escaped the pollutions of the world, not the corruptions; that is, they have been washed on the outside, and have not been changed on the inside.

- They have "head knowledge" of Christ and not a heart of faith.

- They are not truly saved, for they go back to the old life after professing faith for a while.

- They have been reformed but they have never received the new nature.

So a faith that knows, is not a mere surface awareness of the facts about Christ, but a deep genuine personal sharing of life with Christ based on repentance from sin and personal saving faith in Him.

A faith that grows (1:5-8)

The word here is diligent. The child of God is to put forth maximum effort. The life of godliness is not lived without effort. Even though the Holy Spirit is in you --- make every disciplined effort, Peter said, "giving all diligence,"

- Add to your faith – virtue [strength]

- Add to your virtue – knowledge [knowing]

- Add to your knowledge – self-control [self-restrained]

- Add to your self-control – perseverance [endurance]

- Add to your perseverance – godliness [obedience]

- Add to your godliness – brotherly kindness [sacrifice]

- Add to your brotherly kindness – love [fervent]

In verse 8 Peter says, if these things (fruits of the spirit) are yours and are increasing in your life (vv.7-8), a child of God will not be barren, useless or ineffective. When these Christlike qualities are not present in the believer's life, he or she will be indistinguishable from the unregenerate.

> *"Therefore, brethren, be even more diligent to make your call and election sure, for if you do these things you will never stumble; for so an entrance will be supplied to you abundantly into the everlasting kingdom of our Lord and Savior, Jesus Christ" (2 Peter :10-11).*

Assurance is one's confidence that he or she possesses eternal life. In other words, the believer who diligently pursues the spiritual qualities mentioned above guarantees to him or herself by their spiritual fruit that they are called and chosen by God to salvation (see

Romans 8:30; 1 Peter 2:21). He or she will not stumble into doubt or fear but enjoy assurance that he or she is saved.

A faith that shows (vv. 9-11)

> *"And the things that you have heard from me among many witnesses, commit these to faithful men who will be able to teach others also" (2 Timothy 2:2).*

"Him would Paul have to go forth with him," was Timothy's call to service (see Acts 16:3). His mission was to "commit" which means deposit and refers to the truth of God's Word which Paul had committed to him (see 1 Timothy 6:20) and which God had first committed to Paul (see 1 Timothy 1:11). This why Paul refers to the local church "the pillar and ground of the truth" in 1 Timothy 3:15).

God has deposited with His people the truth of His Word. It is our responsibility as the local church to guard and preserve the truth. Many churches treat this passage as if God meant put it away in a safety deposit box. Timothy is to deposit the truth with "faithful men" not just any believer. These faithful men (generic) are to deposit the truth into other faithful men; who in turn will deposit it yet, into others.

I said at the beginning of this chapter, the false teachers are trying to dispel the truth of God's Word. It is every Christian's responsibility to witness about Jesus to others not only with our lips but our life living must be faithful to the Word! Daily we hear of more and more subtle persecution. But we must learn to endure hardship for Christ. This certainly should not be a surprise. We are to expect opposition. Every place we step today is a potential battleground.

Many in the local churches through biblical and spiritual ignorance are going to bow under the coming onslaught. We need to fortify ourselves in the word and prayer; so that we will be able to help others when the results of the 2016 elections are over. The nation as we have known it will have to change no matter which party is in the Whitehouse.

CHAPTER SUMMARY: CHAPTER 14

1. The key word in 2 Peter is _____.

2. Salvation is a personal _____ with Jesus Christ.

3. We must have a faith the _____,
   _____ and _____.

4. We must know Christ in a _____ relationship.

5. The Bible can _____ life to our souls.

6. The child of God becomes "partakers of
   _____ _____."

7. It takes much _____ to live the
   life of _____.

8. Without the fruit of the Spirit the child of God is
   _____ from the _____ of
   the _____.

9. It is our responsibility as the _____ _____
   to guard and _____ the truth.

10. We are to deposit the truth with "_____
    _____" who are to deposit the truth to
    _____ _____.

PART II
"WHAT WE DO"

SECTION FIVE

THE RIGHTEOUS

CHAPTER 15

TAKING A STAND

"We do not wrestle against flesh and blood, but against principalities, against powers, against the rulers of the darkness of this age, against spiritual hosts of wickedness in the heavenly places" (Ephesians 6:12).

Satan knows exactly where to look for weak areas in our lives to use against us. When he finds an area in our lives that we have not surrendered to the sanctifying power of the Holy Spirit and the Word of God, he will instantly move to seize any area in our minds or emotions and then brings it to active duty with strongholds to work against our spiritual growth and fruit bearing. That's why we must deal with all sin in our lives. Satan never changes his cunningness and he stalks around day and night.

The warfare center

Satan knows that if he can get a foot hold in any area of your mind; like a cancer, he can spread quickly to other areas that need to be strengthened by the Holy Spirit and the Word of God. Once he's in, his specialty is to corrupt your mind with:

- Unbelief
- Various strongholds
- Wrong thinking
- Wrong believing
- Generational fears and superstitions transferred from our parents, family and others.
- Memories of terrible events that happened prior to salvation
- Incorrect teaching and training of doctrinal truths
- Things [other gods]

We should remember the natural mind is enmity toward God. Therefore, we were all born with rebellious nature and mind against God. That's why we are exhorted throughout the epistles to renew or minds through the truth of God's Word. Satan knows that if your mind is renewed to the truth of God's Word – his efforts will be futile. Not only will the truth set you free but your family also when rightly applied to all! Therefore, if we are going to take a stand our minds must be thoroughly renewed.

Preparation for war

In any warfare be it enemies of the state, competitive sports, or fashions, it is customary to find out what we face and how it works. This holds true also in order for people to be delivered from demonic oppression. The Holy Spirit is speaking loudly concerning this matter these days. Pastors and other church leaders are waking up to the reality of increased intensity in demonic control and manipulation amongst the flock.

In light of this assessment it behooves all of the children of God at all levels to give heed to what the Spirit is saying to the Churches and launch adequate offensives in their areas of influence as guided by the Holy Spirit and truth of God's Word. As we prepare to engage the enemy we must be very careful to walk in balance ourselves. Insure that we are not vulnerable in any area:

- Mortify the flesh (Colossians 3:5)
- Dead to sin (Romans 6:2)

Paul cautions, "Don't live the way you use to live, the way the unsaved lives. Christ is your life, and you died with Him. Now, let His life show through you day by day." I read a story concerning a police captain who sent a young police officer up on a bridge tower to talk a man down who was threatening to jump to his death. The captain was distracted for a moment as he answered a phone call; when he looked back up both men were jumping. The young rescuer was carrying too much of his own excess baggage! He was not able to stand. Satan knew which button to push and when to push it!

Our own day

Living in these postmodern times, it is natural for us to think that our problems are far worse than any generation's prior to this. But even with all our present problems and future difficulties still to come, the situation we face today are really no greater than those of the past generations of God's children who have gone before us.

When the Church was born on the Day of Pentecost, history reflects a world very similar to ours. National borders were being removed as homelands were evaded and occupied by the Roman army, violence in entertainment was popular; and godly morals in the Roman Empire were almost nonexistent. Satan used all these entities as a plan to destroy the Church of Jesus Christ before it could destroy him. Of course his plan failed, as God's own plan emerged. Rather than being destroyed, the Church stood forth in the power of the Holy Spirit and met the challenge! Praise God!

CHAPTER SUMMARY: CHAPTER 15

1. We must surrender to the sanctifying power of the _____ _____ and the Word of God.

2. Once in your mind, Satan's specialty is to _____ your mind with _____
   _____ _____ _____
   _____ _____.

3. We were all born with _____ nature and _____ against God.

4. If we are going to take a stand our minds must be _____ renewed.

5. Pastors and other church leaders are waking up to the _____ of increased _____ control and manipulation amongst the flock.

6. We must _____ the _____ and die to _____ to walk in balance.

7. The situations we face today are really _____ _____ than those of past generations.

8. The Church was born on the _____ of _____.

9. Early Church history reflects a _____ very similar to our own.

10. Why does the Church grow during persecution? Explain below:

CHAPTER 16

EQUIPPED FOR ACTION

"God is a Spirit and they that worship Him must worship Him in Spirit and in truth" (John 4:24).

One of the main facts we face when digging deeply into the Book of Revelation is that God and the devil are seeking worshippers (see Revelation 14:7; 7:11, 14; 13:4). World events today are astounding and people are focusing their attention on a daily feed from the media. Even among our so-called Christian media the message is openly subjective with little reference to what the Bible has to say about the times in which we live.

Personal politics on a world-wide scale, China's economy, Isis and other radical elements seem to be the rule of the day; but biblical revelation gets very little consideration. Few elected officials anywhere USA are bold enough to stand on the truth of God's Word that they know!

The secular consensus *seems* to be ruling the world today through media, education, science and reason. However, God always has the last Word, and He has spoken through His Son, Jesus Christ, why aren't we listening, America?

Who is on the Lord's side?

At times in the Old and the New Testament, God through the man or woman of God had to call the people to make a choice. Time and time again the line has been drawn between those who chose to "worship and serve the beast and his image" and those who "worship and serve God."

Let's realize up front that in the last great battle before Jesus comes back, the outcome of every person's life shall be weighed upon the scale of "worship and serve" in the midst of warfare and battles, to whom will we bow, God or Satan? Yet, we know that this warfare shall end in the establishment of Lord's kingdom on earth (Revelation 11:15); it is important that we realize the *essence* of the battle is the central issue in our warfare today.

Whom will we faithfully worship and serve during satanic attacks and times of temptation today? *It is imperative that true worship and service come forth **now** in the context of our daily living – people will not worship and serve as things get tighter if they continuously cry and complain over the mere skirmishes we face today.*

We can take a great lesson from the Israelites. The Lord's call to worship and service before Him in the wilderness, notice:

> So they said, *"The God of the Hebrews has met with us. Please, let us go three days journey into the desert and sacrifice to the Lord our God, lest He fall upon us with pestilence or with the sword"* (Exodus 5:3).

> And you shall say to him, *"The Lord God of the Hebrews has sent me to you, saying, "Let My people go, that they may serve Me in the wilderness"; but indeed, until now you would not hear!"* (Exodus 7:16).

When Moses first spoke of God's love for the *Israelites*, we read that they *"bowed low and worshipped"* (see Exodus 4:31). But when trials or persecution came, they quickly began murmuring, complaining, and unscrupulous rebellion. Their worship was very shallow and without heart.

This is the same shallowness of worship that prevails in much of the Christian community today:

- When the message is speaking of God's love and care for His people – we bow low and worship.

- But when the pressures of daily living arise, when temptations come, how quick we are to rebel against God.

- Without true worship the soul has no protection of God. God's purpose in the wilderness was to perfect true worship – which is based on the reality of God and not circumstances.

The Lord knows that the heart that will worship Him in the wilderness of affliction will continue to worship in the promised land of plenty.

What comes out of our hearts during times of stress and temptation was *hidden* during the good times; and therefore in warfare worship is a hedge around the soul. A child of God who has mortified the deeds of the flesh and wields the sword of the Spirit will know the enemy. He or she will discern any trap and will stand against the wicked one, as Paul did when a young girl possessed with a spirit of divination by the devil tried to infiltrate, Paul's ministry! She followed after Paul and his associates, crying out, "These men are the servants of the most High God, who shows us the way of salvation. But Paul's spirit was disturbed. So he turned and said to the evil spirit in her, "I command you in the name of Jesus Christ come out of her. And the demon came out the same hour" (Acts 16:17, 18).

Worship at midnight

We can see a close-up a picture of this worship with Paul and Silas in *the* Philippian jail.

> *But at midnight Paul and Silas were praying and singing hymns to God, and the prisoners were listening to*

*them. Suddenly there was a great earthquake, so that the foundations of the prison were shaken; and immediately all the doors were opened and everyone's chains were loosed. And the keeper of the prison, awakening from sleep and seeing the prison doors open, supposing the prisoners had fled, drew his sword and was about to kill himself. But Paul called with a loud voice; saying, **"Do yourself no harm, for we are all here"** (Acts 16:25-28).*

Wrongful arrest, targeting Christians, dislike and violation of my rights are just a few of the charges Paul and Silas could have lodged against the owners of the slave girl of whom Paul cast out a spirit of divination (see vv. 17, 18).

Because with the spirit gone the girl could no longer turn profits for her masters. The magistrate ordered that Paul and Silas be beaten and thrown into the inner prison with their feet shackled in stocks.

The Scripture says, *"at midnight Paul and Silas were praying and singing hymns to God, and the prisoners were listening to them:"*

- Paul and Silas chose to worship (v. 25).
- The other prisoners listened to them (v. 25).
- The earthquake shook open all the doors of the prison (v. 26).
- The keeper of the prison was about to take his own life assuming all the prisoners had escaped (v. 27).
- Paul called with a loud voice, "Do yourself no harm, for we are all here (v. 28).

Rather than do what comes natural, Paul and Silas chose to worship God. In spite of their wounds, and being shackled in the dark, they offered true worship to God.

Wherever the Word of God is exalted, wherever people separate themselves from wickedness and the world, wherever there is true repentance and obedience to the Holy Ghost – there Jesus will always manifest His presence!

As a result of Paul's and Silas' obedience and love for God, their worship activated the following:

- Anointed prayer and singing charged the atmosphere around them and among all the other prisoners for worship.

- The other prisoners so felt the presence of the Spirit, when the earthquake shook the doors opened – they stayed right there. No doubt what they were experiencing in that dark and murky prison was better than the freedom offered by the earthquake's open doors.

- The jailer's question is still reverberating around the world today. "What must I do to be saved?" And the answer Paul gave is the remains the same answer for the conversion of sinners today. So he said, "Believe on the Lord Jesus Christ, and you shall be saved, you and your household" (see vv. 30-31, 34; Romans 10:9-10). That's it folks, believe [fully accept] Christ's work of redemption on our behalf by faith. We were saved by grace through faith, and not anything we've done!

What must I do?

In order to experience what God is doing today, we must cultivate a close intimate relationship with our Lord and Savior Jesus Christ and begin to view all things from a godly perspective. Satan has a tendency of blowing an anthill of a problem or circumstance so far out of proportion that it *now* appears as an impassible mountain. If you find yourself in this situation adjust your perspective and keep your mind on Christ and His promises. Don't be intimidated by Satan!

Even when we are struggling, we should stop and meditate on the fact that I have been born again and now belong to Jesus. He purchased us for His own possession. In doing so, He paid the ultimate price – His life! We must emphasize the fact that in our salvation a divine exchange occurred; Christ, God's Son took our sins in His own body on the cross and credited to our account His righteousness (see 2 Corinthians 5:21). As stated in an earlier section, we are now a new creation *in* Christ (see 2 Corinthians 5:17).

Two words *"in Christ"* form a most profound statement of the child of God's redemption, which includes the following:

- Our security in Christ who bore in His body God's judgment against sin.

- Our acceptance in Him with whom God is well pleased.

- Our future assurance in Him who is the resurrection our life.

- Our participation in the divine nature of Christ, the everlasting Word (see 2 Peter 1:4).

As we begin to serve our Savior, we must understand that God's work is to be done God's way. We must ask for and depend upon His wisdom alone and not on man's wisdom, "For the foolishness of God is wiser than man's wisdom, and the weakness of God is stronger than man's strength" (1 Corinthians 1:25).

As you serve the Lord, you will surly experience increasing opposition. When this happens it is imperative that you know who you are, who you are not, and whose you are. Then you need to know who the enemy is that you are facing and truly who us the Lord you are serving.

The enemy always tries to scare God's people and cause them to become incapacitated by fear. It seems that radical Islam, Isis, and home-grown terrorists have almost petrified the world. They are spreading fast and certainly their methods are satanic and gruesome – but God is greater! Together, we are the armies of Jesus Christ. In Him, we are invincible – yet through various strategies, Satan still manages to intimidate some children of God and cause others to bring discouragement among the brethren.

Return to our Church roots

The early church is still our best pattern. The disciples spent three and a half years day and night with Jesus. They were taught by the Master Teacher Himself. He not only taught them, but He also demonstrated it every day. Jesus told the disciples that they would preach the good news throughout the whole world (see Matthew 24:14). After His death and resurrection, Jesus told His disciples to meet Him in Galilee, when He arrived; He found six of the disciples out fishing on the Sea of Galilee, notice:

- They caught no fish.
- Once Jesus arrived and became involved their nets were filled.
- The disciples knew they were told to proclaim the gospel to the people.
- They were not lacking in teaching.
- They were lacking the Holy Spirit.

It wasn't until the disciples were all baptized in the Holy Spirit on the Day of Pentecost that they caught fire for the work of the kingdom. These same men who a short time ago is now performing miracles, signs and wonders everywhere they went. Peter, who is well known for his denial of Jesus, preached the gospel and 3000 people were converted!

The Holy Spirit and the Word

The Holy Spirit and the Word work in tandem. The Bible was given to us to be read, obeyed, and passed on to others. No scripture passage is to be interpreted "by itself," that is, apart from the rest of the Word of God or apart from the Holy Spirit who gave it. The Word of God did not come by the will of men, so it cannot be interpreted by the natural mind. The Spirit gave the Word, and the Spirit must teach us the Word. Carefully study the following passages.

But as it is written:

> *"Eye has not seen, nor ear heard,*
> *Nor have entered the heart*
> *of man*
> *the things which God has prepared*
> *for those who love Him." –* 1 Corinthians 2:9-16

"But the Helper, the Holy Spirit,
whom the Father will send
in My name, He will
teach you all things
that I said to you." – John 14:26

"However, when He, the Spirit of truth, has come
He will guide you into all truth;
for He will not speak on His own authority,
but whatever He hears He will speak;
and He will tell you things to come.
He will glorify Me,
For will take of what is Mine
And declare it unto you." – John 16:'3-14

We thank and praise the Lord that our Bible is true! We can trust it because God gave it to us. The apostles received truth from the Holy Spirit, truth about things to come, and truth about Christ. The Holy Spirit is the source of truth. Then under the guidance of the Holy Spirit they wrote those truths in documents in what is known today as the New Testament. Eternal life for the child of God consists of a growing *knowledge* of the only true God.

CHAPTER SUMMARY: CHAPTER 16

1. Digging deeply into the Book of Revelation we find that God and the devil are seeking _____.

2. Biblical revelation receives very _____ _____ today.

3. In the midst of great temptation to whom will you bow in worship and service _____ ?

4. The secular consensus seems to be ruling the world today through _____, _____, _____ and reason.

5. Worship of God is based on the reality of God and not _____.

6. The child of God who has mortified the _____ of the flesh and wields the _____ of the _____ will know the enemy.

7. Paul and Silas chose to worship while in jail rather than _____ or _____ in spite of their wounds.

8. The Word of God did not come by the will of men, so it cannot be _____ by the natural mind.

9. The apostles received truth from the Holy Spirit – for the Holy Spirit is the _____ of truth.

10. Under the guidance of the Holy Spirit the apostles wrote those truths in documents what is known today as the _____ _____.

CHAPTER 17

THE DIVINE NATURE

*"Whereby are given unto us exceeding great and precious promises: that by these you might be **partakers of the divine nature** having escaped the corruption that is in the world through lust"* (2 Peter 1:4).

The Fayetteville Times carried an article this morning by a retired Army General stating that we lost the war on Global Terrorism. Yet, we are still engaged and sending our service personnel out daily to carry out and/ or support life-threatening Global Counter-Terrorism missions. I can't help but wonder what affect the soldiers carrying out these missions on this present Saturday morning, if he read that commentary by a General Officer, whose latest book supposedly tells: Why We Lost!

On the other hand, one of our most noted Christian television personalities begins each daily broadcast with a barrage of uncensored name calling and descriptive terms through gnashed teeth such as stupid, idiotic and you name it against our Commander-in-Chief and his Cabinet Chiefs with smirks and open laughter.

Then we have two nationally known pastors, who are news-makers every time they announce an event the media around the world is interested, why? One of them specializes in desecrating funerals of fallen soldiers, with absolutely no regard for the mourning families. The media searches the words of the second pastor for un-colorful language. All four are speaking subjectively! Where is, "the thus said the Lord?" "Where is the objective biblical prophetic explanation of why *all* of these things are happening to the United States of America?

Why aren't we teaching [truth] that to be successful in any endeavors or decisions-making, God's will, His way and His Word must be incorporated? If God is kicked to the curb and the name of Jesus silenced in the marketplace, it doesn't matter whom we elect as president in 2016 or what programs we initiate. Unless we get connected back with God, we will never be able to fix what's wrong.

However, if we are going to stand for God and His Kingdom agenda – we must get back into the conversation! Secular humanism has made great strides toward destroying this nation over the past one-hundred years. If we bring God back to the center of our lives and stop marginalizing Him and counter the unrighteous rule this nation will return to the favor of God. We are not paying attention Church! Once God is removed from the margins in the culture – He becomes your fiercest enemy and worst nightmare. This is the gist of our problem in America. We are keeping God on the fringes today in a spare-tire mode as a result God is withholding His restraint and we are under His judgment as a nation. I entered the U. S. Army in the 50's. At that time many things began to change:

- God was removed from the Chain of Command.

- Great American leaders began to dwindle [World War II level].

- The military became totally secularly oriented.

- A drought for godly influenced leadership appeared and has increased in from the highest public office in the land down to the local city and town boards.

- Christianity is being squashed by all of the various foreign religions, gods and different beliefs in this country permitted under free speech and freedom of religion.

- America's Christian consensus and biblical worldview has been abolished and replaced with a secular consensus and secular worldview.

- Respect for *all* authority is nil.

- The church in America seems to be going silent.

- Spiritual leadership is being replaced by religious leaders.

For such a time as this

As the children of God, the future of this nation is our Scriptural mission. With all of the chaos, and destruction of individuals, families, churches and communities we can't procrastinate any longer it's time for action. God has provided a picture from beginning to end of what can and will happen if we repent and come back to God before it is too late. Notice,

> *For many days Israel was **without the true God**, and **without a teaching priest,** and **without law** ......*
> *In those times there was no peace to him who went out or to him who came in, for many disturbances afflicted all the inhabitants of the lands. Nation was crushed by nation, and city by city, for God troubled them with every kind of distress.* (2 Chronicles 15:3, 5-6).

Hear what the Spirit is saying to the churches. Three essential entities were missing in the national life of Israel. These same three essentials are missing in America's national life today. Let's take a brief look at each of the three entities:

The true God

Notice the Scripture did not say the Israelites had become secular humanists or atheists or no longer believed in God. The sacrificial fires at the temple didn't go out, but

- Israel had lost their correct view of God.

- The nation was no longer accomplishing His agenda.

- They wanted a God they could control.

- They didn't want the true God.

- They didn't want God interfering with their national life.

Like the Israelites, America doesn't want the *true God* in their business especially since His agenda is greater than ours.

The teaching priests

This text did not say there were no priests. **But the priests no longer taught the truth:**

- They had traded the truth of God's Word for a compromised, watered-down substitute.

- Worship degenerated to entertainment.

- The temple was no longer the center of community life.

- The temple was no longer the conscious for the culture and people to the true God.

Israel was suffering from a lack of spiritual leaders who honored the truth and authority of God's Word.

The absence of God's law

- Without the law of God, the people had a false worldview.

- When the people begin to operate a worldview based on false information, God begins the removal of His restraint.

- When God is marginalized in the culture, then the righteous standard of God in the society is gone (see Romans 1:18-31).

- When the standard of God's rule is missing confusion fills the vacuum left and that's what is happening in America.

God was the cause,

Israel marginalized God, and the result was destruction. We read, "There was no peace to him who went out or him who came in, for *many disturbances afflicted all the people*" (v. 5). In verse 6, as they kept pushing God further away – conflict on both the local and global levels. Although the Scriptures addressed the conditions in Israel at that time; America stands in the same predicament today almost to the letter. The cause of their troubles once again: *"For God troubled them with every kind of distress"* (v. 6). We had better heed this lesson! If we want restoration in America – we must give our all to God.

CHAPTER SUMMARY: CHAPTER 17

1. Unless we connect back with God, America's _____ will never be _____.

2. Three essential entities listed in 2 Chronicles 15:3, 5-6) were missing in the national life of Israel. These same essentials are missing in the American national life today. List below:

    1.
    2.
    3.

3. Without the _____ of God the people had a false _____.

4. Israel marginalized God in the culture and the results were _____.

5. The temple was no longer the conscious for the _____ and people to the true God.

6. America stands in the same _____ today almost to the letter.

7. If we want restoration in America, we must turn it all _____ to God.

8. Briefly define a biblical worldview in the space below?

9. When God is rejected by a society, He becomes their _____ _____.

10. The priests were no longer _____ the _____.

CHAPTER 18

UPON THIS ROCK

"...........And I say unto you, that you are Peter,
and upon this rock I will build My church; and the gates
of hell shall not prevail against it" (Matthew 16:18).

Christ made an important two-point declaration to Peter and
any child of God who is discouraged about their local church,
or some sinning saint can take heart. Jesus said,

"Upon this rock [Himself], I will build My Church,
and the gates of hell shall not prevail against it."

First of all Jesus does not promise to build His Church upon Peter,
but upon Himself, as Peter himself acknowledges in 1 Peter 2:4-9).
One of the first points we should clarify is the fact that every church
in your town or city is not built by Christ and all are not built on the
Rock [Christ], therefore the gates of hell has already invaded, maybe
even founded that church. The Greek word for church is *ecclesia* from
ek," *out of*" and *klesis,* "a calling" meaning: an assembly of called-out
ones.[14]

Christ said, "I will build My Church," which further is described as "the Church which is His Body" (see Ephesians 1:22; 5:23); a company of professed called out believers (see Acts 20:28; 1 Corinthians 1:2; Galatians 8:1.

How well are we doing at what we do

The church is in one of the most strangely mixed periods of history. The picture is full of contradictions. Some observations may be made regarding the ever-changing situation. Despair has settled over the non-Christian population, as their false gods and unsupported philosophies are failing them on every side. As I shared in PART I these times are very similar to the times of Christ's first advent.

The vacuum left actually is an open door for the true gospel. This is a time of opportunity when:

- It is a time of ferment
- Foundations are being shaken
- Doors of opportunity are flying open unexpectedly [everywhere].

Encouraging signs

Many theologians and church historians have described our times as the greatest opportunity for the body of Christ in the past one hundred and twenty-five years.

There are encouraging signs of "grassroots" level revival in many local churches and in the lives of individuals today. Leaders are realizing first-hand that their schemes, programs, and compromised preaching are not working for the kingdom as the pews grow empty.

It's ironic as more and more people are seeking a dynamic spiritual life; at the same time many churches are divorcing the Holy Spirit and His ministry for a laid-back program and entertainment model. Correct doctrine is not enough it does not satisfy if people are not finding the kind of spiritual life Jesus spoke of as recorded in the New Testament.

There is a fast-growing cultural church emerging today that if not careful will almost wipe out the churches mission of evangelism and

159

edification. First of all not only has this "so-called" progressive church divorced the Holy Spirit, but has eliminated the first work of the necessity of being "born again." People are allowed to join the church in an unsaved condition with a possibility of salvation happening some time later; meanwhile their ungodly lifestyles are overlooked and permitted to continue in the name of "moral relativism" "inclusively," "tolerance" and political correctness. Jesus said to Nichodemus, "You must be born again" (John 3:3).

The Holy Spirit's assignment

We cannot know and understand the spiritual life or Spiritual truth apart from the work of the Holy Spirit in our lives. Spiritual truths can be *revealed* only by God:

> *"Eye has not seen, nor ear heard, nor have entered into the heart of man the things which God has prepared for those who love Him. "But God has revealed them to us through His Spirit. For the Spirit searches all things, yes, the deep things of God .... no one knows the things of God except the Spirit of God. Now we have received, not the spirit of the world, but the Spirit who is from God, that we might know the things that have been freely given us"* (1 Corinthians 2:9-12).

The Holy Spirit has the assignment of revealing spiritual truth to the children of God:

- The Holy Spirit is called the "Spirit of truth" (John 14:17, 15:26; 16:13).

- Jesus said the Holy Spirit would "teach you all things, and bring to your remembrance all things that I said to you" (John 14:26).

- "He will guide you into all truth; for He will not speak on His own authority, but whatever He hears He will speak; and He

160

will tell you things to come. He will glorify Me, for He will take of what is Mine and declare it to you" (John 16:13-14).

The Holy Spirit was given to us on the Day of Pentecost. You understand spiritual truth because the Holy Spirit is working in your life. You can never understand the Word of God unless the Holy Spirit of God teaches you. When you come to the Word of God, the Author Himself is present to instruct you. You never discover truth; truth is *revealed!* An encounter with the Holy Spirit is an encounter with God!

It is not strange [knowing that Satan has but a short time] that he would cause as much confusion as possible in the church concerning the Ministry of the Holy Spirit. As I stated earlier, many churches and individuals are selectively not hearing what the Spirit is saying today. Disobedience can lead to a "famine" ...... of hearing the Words of the Lord" (see Amos 8:11-12). If you hear what the Spirit is saying and put into action every word from the Lord by making all necessary adjustments in your life – then God can do in you and through you everything He says to you!

Give me the simple life

People desire the simple, power of the gospel and transformation of the Holy Spirit idealized in the New Testament. Interest in traditional denominational conventions and other religious causes along with ecumenism is waning. In fact anything above the local church level [grass roots] is unacceptable to many local churches. The local church and more specifically the *individual Christian,* is the focal point of the kingdom. Fellowshipping with churches across denominational lines has become the norm among true Spirit-filled children of God. Whatever happens at the local level is ultimately important:

• Interest in "good" teaching is on the increase. This is the kind of message that plugs into today's lives and needs connecting them to the power supply of the **truth** of God's Word. My wife and I founded the Bread of Life Bible Institute 1998 for the express purpose supplying [teaching] only the truth of God's Word. We are a non-traditional school where we tailor the courses to meet the spiritual and biblical needs of the people in the area. God has blessed us with multi-campuses in located in five states. Our motto tells it all, "Come Learn – Go Teach!" I believe that this effort by churches and Para ministries all across the world are going unreported, for several reasons:

1. We are non-accredited by choice.
2. We are non-denominational, which allows us to work strictly with the truth of God's Word.
3. There are no salaries.

• Many people are discouraged by the great divide between those in the church who only hear the truth, but do not heed it; yet I believe those who hear and live out the truth under the guidance of the Holy Spirit in their daily experiences and interaction with others are on the rise.

The image many people have of the church, a collection of nice inflexible people, who memorialize their patriarchs and matriarchs on little plaques honored with candlelight services and recommitment to hold fast to the traditions, customs and programs as passed down by their founders. This signifies that "we do not change." "That's just the way it is." Of course this picture would be provided by the media.

Eventual change

Church history reveals that the churches do eventually adapt to cultural change. There are many noticeable cultural changes impacting the existing church:

• Taking priority is evidence as the number of church plants increases.

• The development of alternative services in more traditional churches.

• The major media attention directed toward these changing ministries.

162

- Many more of the true children of God [all age groups] are at work in this generation.

- Small group ministries are thriving. The traditional churches seem to be opening up for innovation. I encourage some groups that would leave the church with their ministry to stay there and strive to make it a part of the church.

They'll do fine and whatever is required of them will be accomplished through the leading of the Holy Spirit and obeying the Word of God. Rest assured, God will pour out His Spirit on those whom He has truly chosen and called, just as He has done in prior generations.

In an earlier chapter, I addressed Israel's demise due to three missing functions (2 Chronicles 15:3, 5-6) in their religious life:

- Without the true God.
- Without a teaching priest.
- Without law.

America is rapidly moving in the same direction as ancient Israel. The Scripture said, "......... *for God troubled then with every kind of distress*" (v. 6). I believe God is troubling America with all kinds of distresses. We can see it in the weather, storms, economies, lack of effective leadership. He has withdrawn His restraint in some areas. Much prayer goes up when we are involved and then it dwindles; however we are seeing national and international crises and incidents affecting the world.

The problem is still the same [no God]

The apostles John and Paul were given great insight into the condition of the church of the last days of this age. Many of our religious leaders are leading their people to the politicians for an explanation for these perilous times that we find ourselves in. As a result, they are leading their congregations in support of secular policies and laws that are in direct violation of God's Moral Law.

Some are even striving to influence by promoting a specific political philosophy, conservative or liberal; Republican or Democratic, etc. These are all alternatives to the truth of God's Word. In His Word, the Lord made it very clear and simple what will happen to nations and people who turn their backs on Him.

America is rapidly slipping into apostasy and Christlessness willingly; rather than repenting and turning to the Lord for salvation and to our Creator, the only true and living God. So there we have it, life in America is becoming more perilous – because Americans are becoming less godly as our churches descend deeper into the secular culture!

Without God and Christ

Perilous means difficult, hard, violent, troublesome, uneasy, and dangerous days at the end of the present age. Paul painted a picture through prophesy some two thousand years ago of the days just before Jesus returns sometime in the future, the days would be perilous. He pointed out some eighteen identifying characteristics of the people of those days (see 2 Timothy 3:1-4).

The characteristics signify what they "are" in the culture, wider society and what they are "doing" to cause the times to be perilous:

1. People will be *lovers of themselves;* this is not the normal, but selfish, self-centeredness. Self-love sets you up as a god unto yourself (see Matthew 25:43).

2. People will be *covetous.* This means lovers of money and possessions. They are seldom happy with what they have (see 1 Timothy 6:10).

3. People will be *boasters,* braggarts, pretenders. They boast on what they have (see Romans 1:28-29, 30).

4. People will be *proud.* That means they will exalt themselves, and put self before others (see Matthew 23:12).

5. People will be *blasphemers.* They will slander, insult, revile, reproach, and curse others (see James 3:8-9).

6. People will be *disobedient to parents*. They will refuse to do what parents tell them; rebel against parents, and disrespect them (see Ephesians 6:1-3).

7. People will be *unthankful*. They will show no sense of gratitude or appreciation for what a person has and receives (see Romans 1:21).

8. People will be *unholy*. They will be profane, indecent, shameless, and given over to the most base passions (see Luke 1:74).

9. People will be *without natural affections*. They will be abnormal in their affection and love. There love will be cold toward God, Christ, the Holy Spirit and the children of God (see Romans 1:21).

10. People will be *trucebreakers*. The will break promises and agreements; faithless, treacherous, and unfaithful (see Ephesians 4:25).

11. People will be *false accusers*. The Greek word *diabolos*[15] and used 34 times as a title of Satan, the Devil. Also slanders (see 1 Timothy 3:11; 2 Timothy 3:3).

12. People will be *incontinent*. This means the person is undisciplined and cannot control his or her passion for food, sex, pornography, drink, drugs, smoking, or whatever. It becomes an unbreakable bondage requiring deliverance (see Romans 6:12).

13. People will be *fierce*. That is they will be savage, untamed, unrestrained, in its fierceness. Never before have humans become as fierce as they are today. They don't just murder, they mutilate, and torture taking pleasure in it (see 1 John 3:15).

14. People will be *despisers of those who are good*. These people will despise good people and good things. Those who stand for truth (see 2 Peter 2:10).

15. People will be *traitors*. I refers to a person who betrays a trust to a person, their country, or friends (see James 4:17).

16. People will be *heady*. They will be headstrong, rash, and reckless. This person know what's best, the consequences are of little importance (see Ecclesiastes 5:2).

17. People will be *high-minded*. They will be puffed up, conceited and feeling self-important. It is a person who feels so educated, so advanced.so high in position, authority, and gifts make them feel completely sufficient (see Romans 12:16).

18. People will be *lovers of pleasure more than lovers of God* (Romans 12:3). That is a carnal mind and full of enmity against God. These persons prefer anything before Him especially carnal pleasure.

Watch your life

Every child of God must constantly be on the look-out for the dangerous roadblocks and signs that the Lord told you will come. I'm sure that you agree that these characteristics are similar to our own nation. The wise person will heed the warning and make the necessary corrections in the course of his or her life before it's too late:

- Are you looking ahead or being caught unware?

- All of God's children must be prepared "to stand" against the godless behavior of the people and the wiles of the devil, in both the present days and the last days!

- To experience God's ever-available power "to stand", you must open your heart to Him and ask that it be released in your life. By *faith* you must reach out and embrace this special power (see Acts 1:8), for because of your position "in Christ" you are surrounded by it at this present moment. Reach out and grasp and exercise the promise!

CHAPTER SUMMARY: CHAPTER 18

1. Jesus promised, upon this _____ I will build My _____.

2. A church is defined as a company of professed _____ out _____.

3. Many churches have _____ the Holy Spirit.

4. People desire the simple _____ of the gospel.

5. Interest in good _____ is on the increase.

6. List the three missing functions in 2 Chronicles 15:3, 5, 6:

   a.
   b.
   c.

7. Perilous times means _____ and _____.

8. Blasphemer means _____.

9. Define high-minded below:

10. What is the challenge for every child of God in reference to _____ and signs.

SECTION SIX

WALK IN THE SPIRIT

CHAPTER 19

THE CHURCH OF THE LIVING GOD

*"But you shall receive power when the Holy Spirit
has come upon you; and you shall be witnesses to Me in
Jerusalem, and in all Judea and Samaria, and to the
"end of the earth"* (Acts 1:8).

God created the church and commissioned it as the means
through which He presently pursues His eternal purpose in
the world. The church then, can expect Him to provide all of the
necessary power and resources for any assigned task. He willed its
existence before the foundation of the world:

- He provided for its activation through the death, burial, and
  resurrection of His son, Jesus Christ.

- He brought it into being through the power of the Holy Spirit
  on the Day of Pentecost (see Acts 1:1, 4, 8).

- He gave the church the commission to make disciples of His
  Son through evangelism and edification.

In the commission, Jesus promised, *"And surely I will be with you always, to the end of the age"* (Matthew 28:18-20). All of the children of God have this assurance when engaging and carrying out any task assigned. In Christ's mission to the world, we preach, teach and witness, but it is God who has given the gospel, which is His power unto salvation (see Romans 1:6). Paul explains to the Thessalonian Christians,

> *"Our gospel did not come to you in word only, but also in power, and in the Holy Spirit in much assurance........"* (1 Thessalonians 1:5).

In like manner he reminds the Corinthian Christians,

> *"I was with you in weakness, in fear, and in much trembling. And my speech and my preaching were* not *with persuasive words of human wisdom, but in demonstration of the Spirit and of power, that your faith should not be in the wisdom of men but in the power of God"* (1 Corinthians 2:3-5).

Paul wanted to model Christ's humility to the rich and gifted Corinthians by presenting his "weaknesses" Then the "strength" of the gospel message could be clearly seen. In (Philippians 3:4-9), we see that Paul had many strengths of his own – but he wanted to be counted among those who relied on God's strength. The necessity for God's indwelling and empowering of His people has not changed! The true Spirit-filled children of God and Churches know that God is at work today and that He is involved with them in accomplishing His will. Without His power they cannot achieve anything!

The present day

The potential for the Spirit's supernatural power in doing great exploits for the glory of God remains a great unexplained and unexplored frontier for many Christians and local churches alike. Many communities of faith seldom witness experiences beyond the natural parameters.

All too often local churches demonstrate only those accomplishments operating on the earthly level of "that's just the way it is!" Whatever is accomplished is:

- Done on the basis of human wisdom, resources, ingenuity, and efforts alone.

- Done using plans, decisions reached as if it were up to them.

- Done as if there is absolutely no potential outside of themselves really existed, as if God is off somewhere doing bigger and better things.

- Done as they repeat the words about the power of God, but do not act on the truth of them.

It has been said, "If God ever went out of business; some churches would never know the difference." Most churches probably do not totally neglect the divine power of God available to them, but only a few utilizes it. Why does this happen? It occurs for several reasons:

1. Many of the church members may be biblical and spiritually ignorant of what God's purposes and will really are. More and more religious organizations have a shallow of the authority of Scripture. Thus, the Bible has been neglected in the home, pulpit, and church schools.

2. Those Churches whose members lack an operational biblical worldview, do not pursue God's commissions of evangelism and edification.

3. Church members may be intellectually aware of the preaching and teaching of Scripture, but fail to act on it because they lack faith in the God of the Bible themselves.

4. Many local churches fail to act on the Great Commission although their members understand God's working in the

world to save humans and develop them into mature disciples. Yet, they believe they have no active part to play in all of this.

Certainly these problems are not new. Some of churches in the first three chapters of Revelation had become apostate in varying degrees:

- Sardis had the appearance of life, but the Lord said, it was a dead church. Although it had a reputation, the appearance of success, and outward façade – Christ still judge them to be a dead church.

- Laodicea was content with a shallow religion, but divorced of the Holy Spirit, thus demonstrating how easy it is to be religious, academically and theoretically then fall into formal but dead orthodoxy. Religious but lost!

While some churches do not actively approach God's purposes, others fail to experience the fullness of God's power, because:

1. They pursue His purposes with a *humanistic* attitude of self-sufficiency rather than one of dependence on God.

   Many contemporary churches in America are especially susceptible to this humanistic attitude because of the way our culture idealizes the independent, *self-made individual.*

2. The secularly-imbedded humanistic/ atheistic cultural influence has subtly tempted many Christians to believe that he or she should be able to accomplish their duties on the strength of their own human abilities.

   Likewise, many local churches in America believe that they can complete their commitments to God if they can build up their attendance numbers. Their confidence is in the *power of numbers,* the hidden resource of the *human spirit,* and the possibilities of a *determined will.* Notice the subtle non-presence or necessity of God, Christ or the Holy Spirit.

In their desperate attempt to create new and effective ways to disciple people, they have lost their necessary sense of *dependence upon God for all things,* including the fulfillment of His commands and commitments. The problem with such individuals and churches is not ignorance of God's purposes per se – but ignorance of their own short-coming when they seek to fulfill His purposes without the Holy Spirit's presence and empowerment. Both situations deprive churches of the kind of spiritual power God wants His children to experience and enjoy.

This confusion has placed many Christians and churches right in the middle of a satanic deception. In these churches generation after generation have followed the traditions and customs of the fathers; so they find themselves convinced that their way is the true way. These churches commonly hold their image as one of defense and security. The enemy, to them is on the offensive, as a raging lion against God's people, seeking to defeat them – but the church is secure within God's purpose – the church is safe!

In order to achieve results greater than mere human effort could ever produce; serious Bible study and prayer must occupy a position of the highest priority in the church and lives of its people:

- Through Bible study the church and the children of God perceive God's purposes more clearly. Additionally, each member has the opportunity for oneness in Christ as they acquire a viable biblical worldview to be shared by the entire membership.

- Prayer too is imperative in the development of spiritual life in the church as well as in the personal life of each member. Without consistency in our prayer life, we operate on our own natural resources as we find our spiritual resources completed extinguished.

The great Polish pianist, Paderewski, used to say that if he stopped practicing for one day he noticed it. If he stopped practicing for two days, his family noticed it. If he stopped for three days, the public could tell the difference.[16] If the child of God stops practicing the presence of God in regular prayer, he or she finds:

- Their heart becoming cool.
- Their spirit insensitive to the words of those around them.
- Their compassion dries up.
- Their urgency of their mission in the world subsides.

The truly Christ-oriented individuals and churches hold a more appropriate image, in which the church *aggressively pursues the victory!* In the right orientation and image the *enemy* is the one who retreats and seeks the hiding position. God provides armor and weapons for His children and churches to take the offense.

CHAPTER SUMMARY: CHAPTER 19

1. God created the church and commissioned it as a means through which He presently pursues His _____ _____ in the world.

2. God activated the church through the _____ and _____ of His Son, Jesus Christ.

3. We are to make Disciples of Christ through _____.

4. Paul wanted to model Christ's humility to the rich and gifted Corinthians by presenting his "_____" so that the "_____" of the gospel message could be clearly seen.

5. Many communities of faith seldom if ever witness _____ beyond the _____ parameters.

6. Churches wherein the members lack an operational biblical worldview do not pursue God's commission of _____ and _____.

7. Many churches fail to experience the _____ of God's _____.

8. Many churches in America think they fulfill their commitment to God by the power of _____ which is the hidden resource of the _____ spirit.

9. Through Bible study the _____ and the _____ of God perceives God's purposes.

10. _____ is essential in the development of spiritual life in the church as well as the personal life of each member.

CHAPTER 20

SOLDIERS OF THE CROSS

"For though we walk in the flesh, we do not walk according to the flesh. For the weapons of our warfare are not carnal but mighty in God for pulling down strongholds" (2 Corinthians 10:3, 4).

Born again, Spirit-filled believers are soldiers in the greatest army ever – the army of the Lord! Each one is under the banner of Christ our Redeemer, and as such opposes and resists all forms of sin and evil, regardless of where such evil is found. However, the believer looks for his or her conquest only through the truth of God's Word by the power of the Holy Spirit, who abides in the bosom of every true child of God (see Romans 8:9, 14, 16).

Fighting from victory

Fighting from victory begins with our thinking. We must have a renewed mind. Most people seem to fear Satan more than they fear God. Their thoughts are on him doing something to them. Much of this comes from the idea that the Christian is challenged by him physically. With all of the sin and sinners in the world – many think he is actually winning – giving the impression that he has overwhelmed us.

A renewed mind would say Jesus won the battle on Calvary. So though Satan roars like a lion; Jesus has already pulled his teeth! That's why he tries to keep the Christian at bay with fear. Fear negates faith! Peter assures by admonishing us,

> *"Blessed be the God and Father of our Lord Jesus Christ, who according to His abundant mercy has begotten us again to a living hope through the resurrection of Jesus Christ from the dead, to an inheritance incorruptible and undefiled and that does not fade away, reserved in heaven for you, who are kept by the power of God through faith for salvation ready to be revealed in the last time"* (1 Peter 1:3-5).

The Greek word translated inheritance here suggests both the future reality and the here and now. God has set aside in heaven a wonderful inheritance that is waiting for His children. God knows those who are His and He keeps them safe from external attacks and safe within the boundaries of His kingdom. Peter further reinforces our faith in what we as His children truly have in Christ and His resurrection victory,

> *"Grace and peace be multiplied to you in the knowledge of God and of Jesus our Lord, as His divine power has given to us all things that pertain to life and godliness, through the knowledge of Him who called us by glory and virtue, by which have been given to us exceedingly great and precious promises, that through these you may be partakers of the divine nature, having escaped the corruption that is in the world through lust"* (2 Peter 2:2-4).

Peter sees grace and peace as blessings that we receive from the knowledge of God and Jesus Christ. This knowledge is not the familiar garden variety common to humanity, but this is a special kind of knowledge, a kind that is complete. Since our knowledge of Christ grows as we mature in "the faith" we will experience His grace and peace many times in our walk with Him. Paul would identify the "divine power" here as *"the power of the resurrection"* (see Philippians 3:19; 4:13). Peter stresses three resources for godly living:

- Divine power – is the power [the Holy Spirit] that God used to raise Christ from the dead and that same power is available to the church today; and has provided the children of God with the spiritual ability to live godly (see Ephesians 1:19-20).

- Divine nature – is the nature that characterizes God, the nature that is expressed in the fruit of the Spirit, righteousness and love in the child of God (see John 1:14, 2 Corinthians 5:17; Galatians 5:22, 23).

- Great and precious promises – refers to the numerous offers of divine provision found through the Scripture. The Holy Spirit is within us as Christ promised (see John 14:13), He will enable us to become increasingly Christlike (see 2 Corinthians 3:18).

We should make our escape from this world by our godly behavior and our renewed mind: "And do not be conformed to this world, but be transformed by the renewing of your mind, that you may prove what is that good and acceptable and perfect will of God (Romans 12:2). With a mind renewed by the knowledge of Christ [the truths of God's Word] rather than being conformed or molded by the world, we are to be transformed by the Word of God. Transformation begins in the heart and mind:

- A mind dedicated to the world and its concerns will produce a life of turbulence "tossed to and fro" by the currents of the flesh and culture.

- A mind dedicated to God's truth will produce a life that can stand the test of time. We can resist the temptations of our culture and wiles of the devil by meditating on God's truth and letting the Holy Spirit guide and shape our thoughts and behavior by it. We are now fit to fight from victory in Jesus!

The Spiritual war [A matter of perspective]

"Finally, my brethren, be strong in the Lord and the power of His might. Put on the whole armor of God, that you may be able to stand against the wiles of the devil" (Ephesians 6:10-11).

Paul knew there is an ongoing experience with God's power that is available to all true children of God. He also knew that we desperately need this special anointing of supernatural power in order to be successful in combating the attacks that the enemy brings against us in this life.

Without the supernatural power of the Holy Spirit operating in us, not one of us can ever be a match against the wiles of Satan or against the demon spirits that come to war against our souls. Satan is well aware of the fact that his power is no match against the power of the Holy Spirit and again, be sure he knows it.

Satan was a powerful and brilliant angel named Lucifer assigned to duties in the very presence of God before he fell into his present state of perversion. And although in a fallen state, he still retains much of his former intelligence and other faculties that were originally given to him by his Creator, God. Jesus stripped Satan of his legal authority over us, however his intelligence remains intact. He is cunning, sharp, and he uses his brainy mind against us today.

The battlefield is our minds

Satan failed in his bid for supremacy, but in his twisted mind, he seeks to outwit our natural minds with his strategies and mind-games he has invented with his incredible intelligence. God's special empowering from on high through the Holy Spirit within us; we are empowered to deal from victory with the archenemy of our souls. That's why the Apostle Paul commanded the Early Church to receive this special power – and now the Word of God commands us. This power can be obtained only through a personal relationship with the Lord Jesus Christ; so we must be "in Christ." Ephesians 1:19, 20 declares, that when God raised Jesus from the dead, He used the same power.

When the empowering presence of the Holy Spirit is operative in our spiritual lives, we can engage in battle with the enemy. We do not have the strength in ourselves to carry the heavy armor of God; that we must have in the campaign against the *wiles* of the devil.

The wiles of the devil

We are told to, put on the whole armor of God, that we may be able to "stand against" the wiles of the devil. What are the wiles of the devil – that requires the whole armor of God to combat?

The word *"wiles"* taken from the Greek word *"methodos"* denotes "craft, deceit" (*meta* "after," *hodos* "a way"). The KJV paraphrases it, "they lie in wait" (to deceive).[17] When considering this word "wiles," we see that we must know the devil's strategy to attack and victimize the human mind. Why the mind? Whoever controls a person's mind also controls that person's health and emotions; and knowing this, Satan seeks to penetrate a person's intellect; so he can flood it with *deception*. Once this is accomplished he can begin to manipulate that person's body and emotions as the controller.

Once Satan arrives "after paving a way" the process of mental and spiritual captivity of the person's life is well on the way. What happens next is up to the person who is under attack. He or she can throw off this process:

- By renewing the mind with the truth of God's Word.
- By allowing God's power to work within him or her.

Otherwise it will not be long before a stronghold of deception begins to dominate his or her self image, emotional status, and overall thinking. *Deception* occurs when a person *believes* the lies that the enemy has been telling him or her.

The instant someone begins to accept Satan's lies *as truth* is the instant those wicked thoughts and mind games begin to produce the devil's reality in that individual's life. A common deception the devil assaults the minds of many with is continually telling them that God knows it's your time! Then he will wrap that statement up with the cultural slant [tolerance, inclusive, political correctness] on the issue to soften you up. In spite of the truth of God's Word, walking in the flesh *seems* more real and acceptable to many Christians and churches today than walking in the *spirit*. As people *accept* this lie Satan easily sets up his deception in their minds. The sins of the flesh are becoming the norm today – in spite of the abundance of biblical truth, *"those who practice such things **will not** inherit the kingdom of God.*

The unregenerate sinner can only sin, but cannot live holy – the Christian can live holy and sin, but not at the same time.

As stated in an earlier section, *"practice"* alludes to "living in" or a determination that a certain sin is permissible in spite of biblical truth and church policy. Notice these works of the flesh practiced in many churches as *"silent issues:"*

- Adultery – unlawful sex relations outside of marriage (see Galatians 5:19; Matthew 5:32; 15-19).
- Fornication/ Cohabitation – all manner of other sexual relations (Matthew 5:32)
- Uncleanness – all forms of sexual perversion (v. 16; Romans 1:21-32; 6:19).
- Lasciviousness – anything tending to promote sexual sin [pornography has reached epidemic proportion in the churches among both genders today] (v. 19; 2 Peter 2:7).
- Idolatry – passionate affections upon material things (Galatians 5:20; Colossians 3:5).
- Witchcraft – a controlling spirit; dealing with evil spirits (v. 20; Revelation 22:15).
- Hatred – bitter dislike; abhorrence (v. 20; Ephesians 2:15-16).
- Variance – discord, dissensions, quarreling (v. 20; Romans 1:29).
- Emulations – envies, jealousies, outdo others, zeal (v. 20; Romans 10:2).
- Wrath – indignation, fierceness (v. 20; Ephesians 4:31; Colossians 3:8).

- Strife – contentions, pay back (v. 20; 1 Corinthians 12:20).
- Seditions – disorder, parties, divisions (v. 20; 1 Corinthians 3:3).
- Heresies – goes astray from truth (v. 20; Acts 5:17; Galatians 2).
- Envying – jealous of others blessings (v. 21; Matthew 27:18).
- Murders – to kill; hatred (v. 21; 1 John 3:15).
- Drunkenness – living intoxicated (v. 21; Romans 13:13).
- Reveling – rioting; sinful activities (v. 21; 1 Peter 4:3; Romans 13:13).

When the above destructive behavior is portrayed and allowed to flourish in Christians; there is no doubt that he or she is not walking in the power of the Spirit (see vv. 16, 18, 23), but is being energized by demonic influences (see Matthew 16:23; Acts 5:3). If not countered by the Holy Spirit and truth of God's Word, eventually these people will begin to believe Satan's lies concerning the practice of these fleshly sins.

Once the lie is accepted as true, the deception has set in and construction of a stronghold is ready to be planted in the person's mind. Study the example in 1 Corinthians 5, where the church tolerated a known incestuous situation, and allowed it to continue in the church. The church became full of pride, *thinking* that they were pleasing the Lord by being able to tolerate such immorality.

Many churches seem to be modifying their constitutions and by-laws in order to accommodate the secular laws passed through our courts in rejection of God's moral law which is higher than any court in the land to include the Supreme Court of the United States.

This is a crucial time for the church to stand up; and appeal to the highest court of the universe, God Almighty! Praying and counseling with teens is an impossible challenge without the empowerment of the Holy Spirit and truth of God's Word with proper training in wielding the word. That's why it's so important to belong to a Bible-believing church today. This confusion or contamination is diabolically planned and instituted through the secular humanists' agenda today. Let me present just two questions that I have been inundated with:

- Many teens express to me what shall I do, "I don't know what I am?"

- Others express, "I will be glad when I graduate there are just as many girls after me as boys!" "What am I to do?"

Unless the churches see the importance of teaching God's perspective on sexual morality; secular sex education will continue to flourish unchecked among the youth and millennials in our Communities of faith. This one-sided situation will set up many children for experimentation, peer pressure and parental and church neglect leaving the children to fiend for themselves. God forbid! Permissiveness, promiscuity, and sex education as presented in our public school systems would lead students to believe all of this is normal including teen pregnancies, government dependency, abortions and High school dropouts. This early shift from teens to adulthood can be traumatizing as babies have babies producing many targets of opportunity for satanic deception. Then reality sets in as the lies are revealed. Young people in the church are caught up in this web of lies as well as those on the outside, who have little no spiritual or biblical exposure.

Again, once the lie is believed the deception is complete so the stronghold is constructed. We must be mindful at all times that spiritual warfare rages *between our two ears, in our minds*. This person's mind has not been fully transformed. The Spirit has been hindered, probably by the deception of selective disobedience through omission in the church. Christ has always been the answer to all situations and the only way to God – and He remains the answer today! He will transform you and your problems if you turn to Him. Certainly a relationship with Him will quell all of those other voices ringing in your head including your own. There is absolutely no other way to the peace you seek!

Unless these sins are repented of, forsaken and put out of their lives, the Scripture says, they will not inherit the kingdom of God. Silent sins are very destructive as they tear down hedges of protection around the lambs and sheep allowing free passage for wolves in sheep clothing! The point is many churches deny the power of the cross and resurrection of Jesus Christ. They deny [through omission] that Jesus Christ can save people from perishing and give them eternal life.

One of the greatest deceptions in the lives of people today is the blanket acceptance of anyone who simply say they are a Christian. Are we so gullible? Simply saying the words is not enough!

However, "Walk in the Spirit and you <u>shall not fulfill</u> the lusts of the flesh" (study this promise in Galatians 5:16-17). Those demonic allegations will have no power or control in your life. That's a promise!

Preparation for battle

By now we should have discovered that natural weapons to include talking ability, money, politics, education, power and influence will not help us in our fight with these unseen, spiritual enemies. Paul wants us to know of whom our battle is against. He says,

> *"For we wrestle not against flesh and blood, but against principalities, against powers, against the rulers of the darkness of the world, against spiritual wickedness in high places"* (Ephesians 6:12).

Notice the real adversaries are an unseen host of wicked spirits that are working behind the scenes through the devil's children and fleshy Christians. However he can do nothing with the Christian unless we allow the flesh to cooperate with them. These demonic forces come to tempt, seduce, deceive, and assault our flesh and minds. That's why the flesh must be dealt with before we attempt to deal with the devil and his hosts.

By living a sustained crucified, sanctified, we are able to neutralize any attack the enemy tries to wage against our flesh. How is this true? Dead people don't have the capacity to respond to temptation, or deception.

Likewise, the majority of the demonic attacks against us will never succeed if we are living the crucified life and reckoning ourselves to be "dead to sin" daily:

> *"Knowing this, that our old man was crucified with Him, that the body of sin might be done away with,*

> *that we should no longer be slaves to sin. For he who has died has been freed from sin. 'Likewise you also, reckon yourselves to be dead indeed to sin, but alive to God in Christ Jesus our Lord"* (Romans 6:6, 7, 11).

Some writers say *old man* refers to part of us, to be specific, our old nature and our sinful disposition. However, the word" man" does not refer only to a part of an individual; instead, it describes the entire inner person *before conversion,* because the person is connected to the sin nature of Adam. However, that old man was crucified with Christ (see Galatians 2:20).

Simply put, a believer is not the same person he or she was before conversion – a believer is a new creation in Christ (see 2 Corinthians 5:17).

There are two reasons for crucifying the old man:

1. That the body of sin might be done away with.
2. That we should no longer be slaves of sin.

The sinful nature or sin in the believer's life is abolished when the old self is crucified with Christ. Because we are new people, we are no longer enslaved to sin. If you are even considering yourself as participating in spiritual warfare this question has got to be settled! *Christians must not only **know** that they have died to sin (vv. 6-8) and have been made alive with Christ. They must also **believe** it!*

Christ died for sin once for all. He is now alive at the right hand of God. Since the children of God have been joined to Christ in His death and resurrection, they can now believe that they too are alive to God in Christ.

Though believers *in* Christ have died to sin, sin is still a problem. The sin principle is still present and can express itself through the *mortal body* [which is not yet saved], the body that is yet subject to death. The difference is, sin has no right to reign. Thus Paul admonishes the child of God not to *obey* it!

The enemy is looking for those who are weak in faith, ignorant of the Word of God, isolated unto themselves, and not mature enough to **"stand"** in the face of his constant hassling and accusations (see 1 Peter 5:8).

Our churches have many self-disqualifiers in the membership who fit this category and are like sitting ducks for demonic deception. Paul tells us in 2 Corinthians 11:14, *"And no marvel; for Satan is transformed into an angel of light."* His false prophets, false teachers, false apostles, and other demonic deceivers accessing the churches are always set to attack by coming against a person's mind. That is precisely why Peter admonishes us to be, "be sober, and be vigilant, because your adversary the devil, as a roaring lion, walks about seeking whom he may devour" (see 1 Peter 5:8).

Prerequisites for a soldier

In his great love and concern for the Corinthian believers, Paul admonished them of some things they **must do** prior to attempting to put on the whole armor of God. His wise counsel is still fresh and applicable for us, as children of God, today. He urged them to:

- Put away lying (4:25).

- Speak truth with your neighbor (4:25).

- Be angry, and sin not; don't let the sun go down on your wrath (4:26).

- Give no place to the devil (4:27).

- Let him who stole steal no more (4:28).

- Let no corrupt communication proceed out of your mouth (4:29).

- Grieve not the Holy Spirit (4:30).

- Let all bitterness, wrath, anger, clamor, evil speaking, and malice be put away from you (4:31).

We can never afford to forget for a moment that a consecrated life is a prerequisite to true spiritual warfare. If the areas of our lives that Paul mentioned above are left open, un-surrendered, and uncommitted we have left a dangerous breach in our hedge of protection through which Satan will continue to ruin our lives.

CHAPTER SUMMARY: CHAPTER 20

1. Fighting from victory begins with our _____.

2. Peter sees _____ and _____ as blessings we receive from the knowledge of God and Jesus Christ.

3. Paul identified the "divine power" as the "power of the _____."

4. Peter stresses three resources for godly living. List them in the space below:

5. Our godly behavior and _____ _____ give us an escape from the world.

6. Satan's power is no match against the power of the _____ _____.

7. God allowed Satan to retain his former intelligence after his fall from heaven.

8. Whoever controls a person's _____ also controls their health and _____.

9. The _____ and the _____ can do only what we allow them to do.

10. List below, 3 of the 8 things that Paul said the believer must do before attempting to put on the whole armor of God:

    1.
    2.
    3.

CHAPTER 21

FIT TO FIGHT

"You are of God little children, and have overcome them: because greater is He that is in you than he that is in the world" (1 John 4:4).

A medical report I read, stated that our present generation is the first generation wherein the parents will bury their children, rather than the other way around. This is happening because the children are less healthy then their parents' generation. Such things as inactivity, improper diets, and over eating were named among the main culprits.

Standards of fitness [Ephesians 3-6]

The military services, law enforcement, sports, and many other activities have set standards of fitness which must be met in order to be accepted. The proof is in the pudding, as those not meeting the standard will fail and therefore be eliminated because of failure to meet the standards of fitness. Their failure may stem from a variety of reasons, some seen and others unseen. Outward appearance does not tell the whole story.

A school mate and I planned throughout our high school years to go into the military under the buddy system immediately after graduation. So after graduation we signed up and were immediately sent to Raleigh to be enlisted in. First on the agenda once we got there was a through physical exam – a few hours later I was sworn into the Army alone! My buddy was rejected and sent back home because of a heart murmur. That was the end of our buddy system. I had to go it alone.

Similarly, only those who meet the standard of fitness are deemed "fit to fight" and given the whole armor of God (see Ephesians 6:10-20). That's why Paul gave the prerequisite standards in earlier (carefully study chapters 4-5), for God had given him the revelation of Jesus Christ which had not been made known in ages past (see Ephesians 3:1-21). He begins the briefing:

> *"Finally, my brethren, be strong **in the Lord** and the* **power of His might**" (Ephesians 6:10).

This very first passage let's us know that we are going to be given a task that we cannot do ourselves. The child of God must heed what God says in this passage and *he or she must do exactly what God says in order to conquer our spiritual foes in life!* So he gives us a three-fold charge, the instructions, are not given to the world – but to the true children of God:

- Be strong
- In the Lord's power
- In the Lord's might

The Source of our strength

Our strength is found only *in the Lord* – as we live in a dynamic relationship with Him. The Lord is the ONLY source of our strength! Like Paul, our strength comes in realizing *our weakness.* There is no other source that can give anyone the strength to overcome this world with all its trials and temptations and death.

Put on the whole armor of God

We must put on the whole armor of God. Once we are *strong within*, then we are ready for the Lord to clothe us with the whole armor of God:

- The children of God must have the heart to fight.

- The children of God must be strong in the Lord and clothed with the whole armor of God.

- Once the children of God have the presence and power of God within their heart – it is then that they are fit to wage war against the spiritual enemies.

- But note a most critical point: he or she must have on the *whole armor* of God – leaving nothing out.

    If a piece of armor is left off, he or she is exposed to the enemy, and stands a good chance of being wounded or killed.

Paul was in prison and under constant guard when writing the Ephesian church. He was forced to look at the soldier's armor day and night. This gave him the ideal picture of the armor needed by the Christian believer to combat the spiritual forces of evil.

All of the armor is not just passive protection in facing the enemy; but it is to be used offensively against the satanic forces. Remember, the battle is in your mind! It is the Lord who puts the armor on us and fights through us. Be ever mindful of Him!

- The first piece of armor is the belt of **truth,** it is the truth that refutes the lies of Satan exposing his deceptions. The Scripture says, "Satan is the father of lies" (see John 8:44). One of Satan tactics is to get you to question God's truth. "Did God say ......?" "Did He *really* mean what He said?" So in order to counter Satan's lies and accusations, it is imperative that we know the truth of God's Word. We should realize that it is only the truth we know that will set us free. That truth has been available for two thousand years in the Bible, where it will remain if we don't search the Bible for them. The Spirit of truth stands ready to assist us, ask Him (see John 8:32).

- The second piece of armor is the chest plate of **righteousness.** This piece covered the body from the neck down protecting the heart. The believer's heart is focused on the Lord Jesus Christ and His righteousness, and that focus must be protected. The uniform of the Christian soldier is righteousness. As we grow in faith we learn to flee temptation and exercise self-control. We continually respond to the sanctifying truth that God shows us concerning His transforming will for our lives. We are to live a righteous life, knowing that our hope is in Jesus Christ.

- The third piece of armor is to have our feet shod with the preparation of the **gospel of piece.** Isaiah 52:7 says, "How beautiful on the mountains are the feet of those who bring the good news of peace and salvation, the news that the God of Israel reigns!" As we enter spiritual battle, our walk depends upon boots cushioned from the shock of rocks or any other ground obstacles that would slow our progress. When your soul is aligned under the rule of your spirit which is God's order. God will release His peace into your life now that the peace of Christ is ruling your thoughts and conduct. Wherever the Christian soldiers' feet carry them, they share the gospel which firmly grounds a world reeling under the weight of need and conflict.

- The fourth piece of armor is the **shield of faith.** The shield worn by the soldier was designed to protect his body from the fiery darts thrown by the enemy. The darts soaked in a combustible solution and set on fire would serve as small bombs. Satan shoots his fiery darts to wear you down by causing the believer:

1. To question his or her salvation
2. To question his or her call

3. To question if he or she is worthy
4. To question if he or she can really serve
5. To question if the project can really be done
6. To question doubt and wonder
7. To become discouraged, depressed, and defeated

These fiery darts often assault the mind through doubting, and one evil thought after the other, fighting against the will, struggling to get a hold of the mind and subject it to doubt or evil. However, the sign of the Christian soldiers is that of the shield of faith, faith in God – a complete and perfect trust that God will help them to control their mind to conquer the evil doubts and thoughts. The Christian soldier's consciousness of God's presence is so great that *God's presence* itself becomes his or her shield and defense. The Scripture says, God is their help and shield (see Psalm33:20; 84:9).

All sin comes from falling for Satan's lies and rejecting the better choice of obedience and blessings. Note some of the fiery darts Satan will throw at you; and remember the battle is in your mind:

1. Hateful thoughts
2. Unresolved anger
3. Doubts about God and the Bible
4. Doubts about Jesus as the only way
5. Doubts about provision
6. Overwhelming times of depression
7. Inferior among others
8. Embedded false beliefs from significant others

Faith destroys the darts of doubt and deception. By faith we have the mind of Christ (see 1 Corinthians 2:16). By faith we trust the Lord's protection and victory over sin and demonic activity. Claiming God's promises by faith, trusting in His unchanging character, and holding up His truth will deflect and extinguish the enemy's lies. Psalm 91 is one of the child of God's best expressions of faith in battle. We accelerate our faith with the truth of God's Word. Think of the darts that have pieced your life in the past. Which of the many promises of God could have saved you from the wounds you received?

- The fifth piece of armor is the **helmet of salvation.** The helmet covered the head and the mind of the soldier. The head, of course, was the core of a soldier's power to wage war. His thinking capacity was the most important factor in discerning his victory or defeat. Therefore the sign of the child of God is the helmet of salvation (deliverance). He or she must protect their mind and its thoughts, of reaching the world with the glorious news of the gospel of Christ. The helmet of protection that protects the child of God's mind is *salvation.* Unless a person has been saved, his or her mind cannot be protected from the fiery darts of temptation. The unsaved person's mind is focused upon the earth – which is normal for that person's mind:

1. To seek more and more stuff
2. To possess more and more
3. To look at the opposite sex with desire
4. To taste and indulge the good things of the earth
5. To have and to hoard even when others have little or nothing

Having the right mind-set [worldview] is important for the child of God. God knew that the battle for the mind would be ferocious at times. Paul also refers to the helmet of salvation as an expression of hope (see 1 Thessalonians 5:8, 9).

- The sixth piece of armor is the **sword of the Spirit**; we can knock out the devil's defenses with the sword of the Spirit, the Word of God. The Word of God, the Bible, is the only piece of armor that we can hold in our hand. All the others are spiritual. God brought His Word, the Bible from the spiritual realm to the natural realm so that the child of God could handle it. In most places in the New Testament the term "word" is translated *"logos"* in the Greek. God applies His Word (rhema) by making the Word (logos) alive and active in

196

our specific situations. Jesus is our example in Matthew 4:4, 6, 10. His rhema word cut through Satan's lies at every turn with *"It is written."* We are to counter lies with truth; which always wins. The psalmist said, "How can a young man keep his way pure? By keeping it according to your Word....." YOUR Word have I hid in my heart, that I might not sin against You" (Psalm 119:11). The Lord commanded Joshua to meditate on His Word day and night (see Joshua 1:8). The result of Joshua's obedience to the Lord's command is biblical history! Of the six pieces of armor, the sword of the Spirit is the only *offensive* weapon.

Overcoming darkness

When the sword of the Spirit, which is the (rehma) Word of God, is spoken in faith – it is a *terrifying weapon* to the kingdom of darkness. Hebrews 4:12 says, "The Word of God is quick, and powerful, and sharper than any two-edged sword, piercing even to the dividing asunder of soul and spirit, and the joints and marrow, and is a discerner of the thoughts and intents of the heart." Because it is our only defensive weapon, we must know the Word of God! It does more than protect us from the enemy's attacks, it changes the situation, puts the enemy to flight – remember we are fighting from victory!

Dispel Meism

In combat there is no such thing as me, myself and I! I often hear people say, "God has my back." They conclude, He did not give a piece of spiritual armor for that. He does have that soldier's back – but through his or her fellow soldier, saint, prayer partner, buddy, or friend. Certainly the Lord hears and answers our individual prayers, but there are also those situations requiring the "two or three!" In Matthew 18:19-20, Jesus said to His disciples,

> *"Assuredly, I say to you, whatever you bind on earth will be bound in heaven, and whatever you loose on earth will be loosed in heaven. Again I say to you that if two of you agree on earth concerning anything that they ask, "it*

*will be done for them by My Father in heaven. For **where
two or three are gathered together in My name**, I am
there in the midst of them."*

This passage recognizes the presence of the Lord. The sanctuary of
God is the assembly of His saints. His presence in the context of this
passage deals with discipline. God through His Holy Spirit is with
His church to quicken our prayers, to answer petitions, and to guide
in counsel. A check of the Scriptures confirms the fact that sometimes
He stands upon a number of voices in carrying out some public mercy,
because He delights in the harmony of many praying saints and also
because He loves to oblige many in the answer! God is glorified in the
praises of His saints.

Some time ago I read an article on Charles Spurgeon, a great
nineteenth century English preacher, called the "Prince of Preachers"
who preached to thousands in his church, the Tabernacle in London,
England. A reporter attending a service inquired of him the secret to
his successful services leading thousands to Christ. Spurgeon, it said
walked him over to a door leading to the basement; he opened the
door and pointed down to a group of saints on their knees in fervent
prayer.

Pray at all times in the Spirit

The fierceness of spiritual warfare has reached catastrophic
proportion because of such philosophies as "Individualism" and others
forms of separation and disunity in our churches. God seeks the unity
of His saints, the body of Christ! God has already made provision for
America as well as other nations in His Word. Even secular history
bears out His promise-keeping for the skeptics. It seems for the most
part many of our churches fail to realize that imbedded in the midst of
His promises – we find deliverance. Many Christians see the so-called
overwhelming conditions and degradation of the world and their
intrusions into the Christian community and just give up! I firmly
believe that the reason for our Country's downward spiral away from
the will of God and His kingdom plan is the absence of meaningful
prayer in the lives of most Christians and most churches. I am talking

about strong, biblical prayer full of dependence, trust and fervency. It brings transforming change in the churches and in the lives of people.

In the context of putting on the armor of God, Paul moves right into prayer without missing a beat. We are to wear our armor with all kinds of prayers at all times in the Spirit. The weapons of our warfare and prayer are integrally connected.

Like it or not, much of the American population is being held hostage by the deceptions of satanic forces of evil. God did not promise to break bondage such as we see increasing daily through politics, town meetings or humanistic philosophies. We must keep in mind as the candidates begin their pitch for their party's choice for the presidency of the United States. The children of God are looking prayerfully to God for America's deliverance.

God promised that "If My people who are called by My name will humble themselves, and pray and seek My face, and turn from their wicked ways, then will I hear from heaven, and forgive their sin and heal their land" (2 Chronicles 7:14). God's people are to respond in three ways:

1. God's people need to become humble (confess).

2. They are to pray (repent)

3. Come back to Him (turn).

If they did these things – God said He would hear, forgive, and heal!

This promise was directed to the people of God and I believe applies to His children everywhere today. When churches are in corporate intercessory prayer strongholds are torn down, old customs and habits discarded, people become courageous, walls of separation between believers will fall, and relationships restored. Can we pray like that? Certainly! God can change your church through you – as it returns to God's kingdom agenda? Friends and loved ones are brought to Christ!

This will not alleviate the warfare, you still must wear the whole armor of God, but when you stand for battle with this kind of prayer in communion with the Holy Spirit's leading. God does supernatural things. Let the Holy Spirit lead you into an intimate relationship with God, "who is able to do exceedingly abundantly above all that we ask or think, according to the power that works in us "(Ephesians 3:20).

In their book "Experiencing God," Henry T. Blackaby and Claude V. King says, "through an intimate relationship with God – He reveals Himself, His purposes, His ways, and He invites you to join Him where He is already at work. When you obey, God accomplishes through you something that only He can do!"[18]

STUDY SUMMARY: CHAPTER 21

1. We are going to be given a _____ that cannot do ourselves.

2. Paul gave a three-fold charge, not to the world, but only to the true children of God to be. Fill in the blanks:

   1. _____
   2. _____
   3. _____

3. Our strength is found only in _____ _____.

4. A most critical point to all children of God – you must put on the _____ armor of God.

5. Not only does the Lord put the whole armor of God on us, He also _____ through us.

6. In order to _____ Satan's lies and accusations, it is imperative that you _____ the _____.

7. All sin comes from falling for Satan's lies and rejecting the better choices of _____ and _____.

8. _____ destroys the darts of doubts and deception.

9. The _____ of the _____ is the only offensive weapon God gives us.

10. According to 2 Chronicles 7:14, God's people are commanded to do three things:

1. _____

2. _____

3. _____

CHAPTER 22

IN SPIRIT AND TRUTH

"Thus saith the Lord, Stand ye in the ways and see, and ask for the old paths, where is the good way, and walk therein, and ye shall find rest for your souls. But they said, We will not walk therein" (Jeremiah 6:16). KJV

We must never overlook the promises of God in the Scriptures. Many people seem to remember only the few that they accept as favorable to them personally. To conclude this book I want us to consider two of His promises concerning:

• The Spirit of truth
• The prayers of the saints

Both have a direct bearing on the deliverance of this nation, (America)! The swift and powerful movement of the Spirit as recorded in the Book of Acts was not only *initiated by prayer,* but *fed* and *sustained* by prayer. Certainly the Scriptures testify to truth – the outcome of which lies in the hands of the true children of God today!

The prayer of the saints

Intercessory prayer is our only hope as we come to realize; that it is the most powerful and strategic corporate weapon in spiritual warfare. It is this corporate weapon by which the true children of God can reclaim this country for the kingdom of God. Satan has turned up the heat, but so can we turn up the heat on him as we appeal the case for America to the highest court in the universe, God Almighty!

Church history bears out the truth – the church is at its finest when the world is at its worst!

The early church knew the supernatural power of prayer:

> *"These all continued in prayer and supplication, with the women and Mary the mother of Jesus and with His brothers"* (Acts 1:14).

The standard was set back in the Tabernacle. Cod commanded Israel, *"Thou shalt set upon the table showbread before me always"* (Exodus 25:30). KJV

The table was to have on it twelve loaves, to be renewed weekly on the Sabbath day. They constituted a continual *thank offering to God,* and it was referred to as the *bread of presence,* signifying God's presence in the holy of holies. The offering on the table of the Lord *not acceptable unless* <u>the surroundings were holy</u>, the flour was the finest and the frankincense pure. The table was overlaid with pure gold. **Nothing common or unclean was to ever touch the sacred table.** The "meal of the Lord" represented what the people brought to the Lord of their labors and worship. The holy bread touched by no unclean hand, was the Lord's feast. It was to be offered willingly, out of a heart of love and obedience.

I think that we give grace a bad eye by our actions, portraying that anything goes and the idea is in the fact I offered it? God forbid! This constitutes a sweet-smelling savor going up before a Holy God. Is God pleased with what we offer Him in worship? Notice the surroundings were holy or the offering was not accepted. Has God lowered the standard for this generation? No! Are our prayers offered from a clean heart? Those fresh loaves represent Christ, the living Bread [Word], with life-giving power and strength.

The Spirit of Truth

Earlier in the book I expressed my dislike for the redefinition or maybe I should say they use the biblical terms, like "Christianity" with a different meaning as listed among the various religions in America. The term "religion" is defined as the practice a body of beliefs as in the case of Christianity begins with its founder who is alive and ruling and directing His affairs in the world through the Holy Spirit. That marks the distinguishing difference; Christianity was founded and is led by the Living God. Life makes the necessity of a relationship. So the Living God who is the giver of all life requires a relationship with the recipient of that life.

This is not the same with the religions of the world; whose founders are long dead but left a set of beliefs which equates to following certain rituals, traditions ending in undetermined destinies. As I stated in an earlier section, many church leaders prefer to hang on to religion because they have never accepted the ministry of the Holy Spirit or have chosen to divorce Him. Just as the Holy Spirit and His ministries moved across denominational lines; so we find divorces across denominational lines!

As noted in an earlier section, Barna Group research indicated that 25% or one quarter of Americans believes in the existence of the Holy Spirit! That leaves 75% or three quarters unaccounted for. This Spirit-less version of so-called "progressive Christianity" was prophesied by the Apostle Paul as he wrote to Timothy in 2 Timothy 3 as one of the major characteristics of the last days before Christ returns. Those persons of this persuasion are on very dangerous ground. I'm sure that the loss of the Spirit's guidance is the major cause for the tremendous loss of millennial generation, ages 18 to 34. Without the Holy Spirit we are all left with nothing! Reason, science and technology are not enough!

This is the exact reason Jesus told the disciples to return to Jerusalem and wait for the Father's promise of – the Holy Spirit's presence (see Acts 1:4-8). I'm sure that ever since Pentecost, "We don't practice that," has been heard and now in spite of the Reformation across denominational lines with the express purpose of barring the ministry of the Holy Spirit from the churches. However, the Spirit is still here and the result of Him coming upon a believer should be that he or she is introduced to *life in the Spirit.*

In this new dimension every spiritual activity is *energized* and *controlled* by the Spirit of God. The child of God should seek to know all he or she can about the person, ministry, and work of the Holy Spirit revealed in Scripture. From Genesis to Revelation, relative to both the creation and redemption, the Holy Spirit is seen in operation. Out of the twenty seven books of the New Testament, only II and III John have no references to the Holy Spirit. The Old Testament foretold of the coming of the "last days" when the Holy Spirit would be poured out upon all flesh.

The Holy Spirit is not an influence

The Holy Spirit is not to be looked upon merely as an influence. Many believers have been robbed of a personal relationship with the Holy Spirit because of spiritual and biblical ignorance they consider the Spirit to be an impersonal influence, power or energy. There are several reasons why the child of God should not consider the Holy Spirit as a mere influence or an impersonal influence:

- It is contrary to the teaching of the Scripture
- It will hinder worship
- It will hinder proper reverence
- It will hinder relationships

The Holy Spirit performs personal acts

The Holy Spirit could never personally take Jesus' place if He was just an influence. He came to be in person relationship with the disciples that Jesus was in personal relationship with on earth. The Holy Spirit came to be in them what Jesus was personally to them.

The whole life of Jesus as the perfect man was governed by the Holy Spirit and prayer. If Jesus depended upon the Holy Spirit and prayer how much more should the children of God constantly in their own right relationships with the Father do the same. All that God has for us and wants to do in us will only be done by the Holy Spirit operating in our lives.

It is imperative that believers be afforded every opportunity individually and corporately to open their hearts and seek the fullness of the Spirit working in them. I am convinced that the next generation cannot survive spiritually if this generation does not submit to the Spirit's leading and take immediate action to insure that a concerted effort is put forth at every level of church leadership's open display total dependence and submission to the Spirit of God, then commit fully to the spiritual and biblical re-introduction of the Holy Spirit by allowing Him to bring new life into the local churches; insuring that it is done in accordance with the truth of God's Word.

Many pastors no longer give the invitation to discipleship as they fleshly doubt that anyone is interested. Where the Spirit is not welcomed or allowed to minister, please notice just a few actions [a foretaste] that cannot take place in your church without the Holy Spirit. They cannot happen because it is only by Him that these ministries can be accomplished. Notice:

- The new birth is brought about by the Spirit (John 3:3,5-6)
- The Spirit indwells the believer's spirit (Roman 8:9; 1 Corinthians 3:16; 6:17; 1 John 2:27)
- The Spirit gives assurance of salvation (Romans 8:16)
- The Spirit speaks to the believer (Acts 8:29; 1 Timothy 4:1; Revelation 2:7, 11, 17, 29)
- The Spirit opens the believer's understanding to the things of God (1 Corinthians 2:17)
- The Spirit teaches the believer, and guides him or her into all truth (John 16:13; I John 2:27)
- The Spirit imparts life (John 6:63; II Corinthians 3:6)
- The Spirit enables the believer to pray (Jude 20; Romans 8:26-28)
- The Spirit enables the believer to worship in spirit and truth (John 4:23-24; Philippians 3:3; I Corinthians 14:15)
- The Spirit enables the believer to put fleshly deeds to death (Romans 6:13)

- The Spirit produces Christ-likeness in character and fruit of the Spirit in the believer's life (Galatians 5:22, 23)
- The Spirit gives a calling to the believer for ministry (Acts 13:2-4).
- The Spirit guides believers into their ministry (Acts 8:29; 16:6, 7)
- The Spirit empowers the believer to witness (Acts 1:8)
- The Spirit imparts spiritual gifts to the believers as He wills (I Corinthians 12:7-11).
- The Spirit will bring about the resurrection and immortality to the believers' bodies in the last day (Romans 8:11; I Corinthians 15:47-51; I Thessalonians 4:15-18).

Reaching young people today for Christ is totally impossible without the empowerment of the Holy Spirit and the truth of God's Word. Obsolete methodology and resistance to change have caused the generational gap to widen rather than narrow. The Holy Spirit is Christ's representative Head of the Church during this Age of Grace. Without the power of the Holy Spirit we are ineffective witnesses, I really believe that the young people are fed-up with all of the talk without the walk. The fallacy in our generation has been our dependency in the accomplishments of humanity without God. We leaned on:

- Science
- reason
- education
- employment
- money
- things
- pleasure
- inheritance
- church [social/ resume]
- exposed to biblical knowledge [little relationship]
- child rearing [give what we didn't have as children]

Today according to Barna research our young people especially ages 18-34 do not believe in the existence of the Holy Spirit and therefore have little knowledge of His available ministries. This church atmosphere has been created through a so-called progressive Christian culture within the church:

- That embraces moral relativism
- That willingly takes your word for claiming to be a Christian
- That is entertainment and pleasure driven
- That wants mainstream services so we won't offend anyone
- That wants every service and activity scripted, scheduled and controlled – something like 45 minutes of music followed by 10-15 minutes for a planned sermon.
- That wants absolutely no Holy Spirit surprises

In Acts 2:2, we see that the Holy Spirit and Pentecost came "suddenly." His coming was unpredictable. There is absolutely no time programmed for the Holy Spirit's surprises – we rehearse and have our five worship songs and the pastor's sermon timed just right. God forbid! We've got to change! The Holy Spirit is described in the second verse of the Bible (see Genesis 1:2) and His last message in the Bible is found in Revelation 22:17). We must teach about the Holy Spirit and get back to altar ministry in the Spirit – where things happen that *only* God can do! Review the listing above in conjunction with your church. Is the Holy Spirit allowed to have His way in your life and your church? When was the last time you heard a series of sermons from the Book of Acts?

STUDY SUMMARY: CHAPTER 22

1. The powerful movement of the Spirit in the Book of Acts was initiated by _____ and sustained by _____.

2. _____ prayer is our only hope and most powerful weapon in _____ warfare.

3. The church is at its _____ when the world is at its _____.

4. Christ is the living _____.

5. Barna Group research indicated that _____% of American believe in the existence of the _____ _____.

6. The loss of the Holy Spirit's guidance is a major cause of the loss of so many in the _____ generation.

7. The Holy Spirit is not to be looked upon merely as an _____.

8. The new birth is brought about by the _____ _____.

9. The Spirit of truth teaches the believer, and _____ him or her into all _____.

10. The Spirit will bring about the _____ and _____ of the believers' bodies in the last day.

CHAPTER 1

1   W. E. Vine's Greek Grammar and Dictionary (Thomas Nelson Publishers 2012) 261
2   Ibid 415

CHAPTER 3

3   Accessed: https://www.barna.org/barna-update/article/5-barna-update/174-most-adults-feel-accepted 11/18/2014.

CHAPTER 4

4   Watchman Nee, *The Normal Christian Life* (Tyndale House Publishers, Inc. 1957) 42

CHAPTER 5

5   Hugh Halter, *Sacrilege* (Baker Books Publishers 2011) 50

CHAPTER 6

6   W.E. Vine's Greek Grammar and Dictionary: Note: in the various of "sons" and "children" Vine's gives two Greek words, *"tekon"*(children) gives prominence to the fact of birth. The Greek word *"hurious"* (sons) indicate the quality of that to which is connected. The KJV does not discriminate between the two words *tekon* and *huious* Page 261

CHAPTER 7

7   Vine's Dictionary 420
8   Accessed: //www.apologeticspress.org/apcontent.aspx?category=9&article+680 2/17/15.
9   John Dewey, *A Common Faith (The Terry Lecture series)* (New Have: Yale University Press, 1934) cover.
10   Charles Francis Potter, *(Humanism: A New Religion* (New York: Simon & Shuster, 1930) 128.
11   Jay R. Leach, *Grace that Saves* (Trafford Publishing 2014) 108

CHAPTER 14

[12]   Vine's Greek Dictionary 421

[13]   Ibid.

CHAPTER 18

[14]   Vines Greek Dictionary 228

[15]   Ibid. 208

CHAPTER 19

[16]   Robert A. Raines, *(New Life in the Church* (New York: Harper & Row, 1961) 60

[17]   Vine's Greek Dictionary 610

CHAPTER 21

[18]   Henry T. Blackaby and Claude V. King, *(Experiencing God)* (Broadman & Holman Publishers 1998) 2